JOBWISE

150 TIPS TO HELP YOU SURVIVE AND THRIVE IN YOUR CAREER

JOBWISE

150 TIPS TO HELP YOU
SURVIVE AND THRIVE
IN YOUR CAREER

Steve Klein, MBA

JOHN WILEY & SONS CANADA, LTD

Toronto • New York • Chichester • Weinheim • Brisbane • Singapore

John Wiley & Sons Canada Ltd
22 Worcester Road
Etobicoke, Ontario
M9W 1L1

Canadian Cataloguing in Publication Data

Klein, Steve
    JobWise : 150 tips to help you survive and thrive in your career

ISBN 0-471-64387-4

1. Career development. 2. Success in business. I. Title.

HF5381.K57 1999   650.1   C99-932710-0

Production Credits
Cover & text design: Interrobang Graphic Design Inc.
Printer: Tri-Graphic Printing

Printed in Canada
10 9 8 7 6 5 4 3 2 1

Contents

Contents

Preface

I feel I've led a life rich in career experience and learning. Over a 25 year career, I have worked in the corporate fast lane and as a self-made entrepreneur. Through study, consultation, trial and error, and the help of others, I've accumulated a lot of knowledge about surviving and thriving in the career world.

It seemed natural to me to share this knowledge with others. Through two nationally syndicated radio shows, CareerWise and A Motivational Minute, I've been doing just that. The shows have been very successful and, if listener feedback is any indication, the advice very helpful.

The 150 tips in this book are based on the actual radio scripts from these two series. They are meant to be quick to read, easy to digest, and practical to use in your life.

I hope that you are able to benefit from the tips in this book and that you, too, will be able to survive and thrive in your career in the years to come.

Acknowledgements

A special thank you to...

My radio producer and friend, Jim Carr for all the energy, passion, patience, and talent that he showed during the development and recording of the two radio shows that are the foundation of this book.

Greg Southorn and Tony Zweig of CJOJ FM in Belleville for giving me my start as a radio features producer and host.

Chris Magwood and Dave Murphy for helping me put together these scripts in a way that's easy and fun to read.

The staff of CareerWise Inc. for all their support during the development of our first radio show.

Karen Milner and Elizabeth McCurdy, my editors at John Wiley & Sons Canada, Ltd, for their unwavering belief in this project.

Bob Laine at the CHUM Radio Network for helping me syndicate our first radio feature, "CareerWise."

Janis Grantham and Kevin Dee of Eagle Professional Resources Inc. for their generous sponsorship of our second show, "A Motivational Minute."

The hundreds of thousands of listeners across Canada who have tuned us in over the past three years.

My wife, Cathy, and children, Nicole and Alex, for their understanding, commitment, and belief in my dreams and love.

part

ONE

How to Use Personal Promotion to Advance Your Career

There was a time when your career would have been defined by the company for which you worked. But those days are gone, and the advancement of your career is now entirely your responsibility. Just being reliable and putting in your time is no longer sufficient.

The scripts in this section address the need to constantly promote yourself in order to get ahead and stay ahead. You must always be showing people what you are capable of achieving. Your ability to add value to your work will make you a desirable employee or a successful entrepreneur.

These tips are based on real-world examples of techniques that can help you advance your career. They have worked for me, and they work for others.

Use them, and you will find a more open pathway to success.

Play Your Business Cards Right

*Your business cards work only
if they are given to people.*

*Surviving and thriving in your
career means turning your card
into a travelling sales rep...*

L yle, a photographer I've been working with, gave me not one, not two, but three business cards. A-ha! I thought, here's a guerrilla marketer! Lyle's three cards turned me into a sales rep for his business. I put one card in my address file and the other two I gave away to clients of mine that asked if I could recommend a good photographer. So, now Lyle has his business card in the hands of two prospective clients he's never met. That's smart marketing!

Your business cards don't do you any good sitting in the box they came in. Play your cards right and, like Lyle, you'll get more customers.

Master the Art
of Mingling

*The ability to work a room and make small talk
can be a huge asset in your career.*

*Surviving and thriving in your career means
mastering the art of mingling...*

It's important to be knowledgeable and up-to-date
when you mix at company or social events. To network effectively, you have to be able to talk to anyone.

1. If you're in business, you should be reading widely—
   three to four hours a week—including the *Globe and
   Mail*, *The New York Times*, and your local newspaper.

2. You should also be reading general interest or news-
   magazines like *Maclean's*, *Time Magazine*, and period-
   icals in your field.

3. Watch CNN in order to keep up-to-date in current
   events around the world.

Having something interesting to talk about around the
water cooler and in the boardroom will help you get
ahead in your career.

Send Your Boss
a Newsletter

*A personal newsletter is an effective way
of promoting yourself and what you've achieved
to the people you work for.*

*Surviving and thriving in your career means
telling your boss the good news...*

About twelve years ago, my boss at the time, taught me the value of writing a monthly report.

He insisted that each of the people working for him prepare a two-page summary of what they had done to earn their salary in the past month.

I soon learned that these "personal newsletters" were a great way of documenting what I had done for him, my teammates, and the company. In these memos I listed the major projects I'd completed, what I'd done to increase sales and profits, and what I was planning to work on next month.

In the new economy, it is critical to tell other people, especially your boss and your customers, what you've done for them lately. A monthly report is a smart career move.

A Little Help
from Your Friends

*A glowing reference letter can be
one of the most effective weapons in your
career-advancement arsenal.*

*Surviving and thriving in your career means
getting a little help from your friends...*

Common wisdom from résumé experts has it that résumés end with the phrase "references supplied on request." Their thinking is that this information is confidential and should be disclosed only to an employer who is close to offering a position.

But smart job hunters realize that conventional thinking just doesn't work anymore. References are an essential part of every résumé—they promote your skills to a potential employer.

My résumé includes quotes from six different testimonials I've collected. I've chosen each one carefully to prove a specific skill.

Ask customers, fellow employees, and even your boss for reference testimonials—build your collection so it will be ready when you really need it.

Wear A
"Personal Trademark"

Golf superstar Tiger Woods always wears
a red Nike shirt on Sundays.

Surviving and thriving in your career means
wearing a personal trademark...

The key to marketing yourself today is to do things that make you stand out. Wearing a distinctive piece of clothing or jewelry is a clever way of differentiating you from everyone else in the pack—it helps people remember you.

Millions of people now associate a white glove with singer Michael Jackson. And who could forget the Laverne "L"?

A "personal trademark" should be something that fits your personality and the image you want to project. It should be subtle yet obvious. You should be proud of it and wear it consistently.

Develop a "personal trademark." Wear it every day and you'll stand out.

You Have to Plan to Win!

If you want to succeed... you have to plan to win!

Surviving and thriving in your career means planning for success...

Doctor Robert H. Schuller says that "Nothing is impossible... you just have to Plan Longer, Plan Smarter and Plan Bigger."

Successful people are successful because they prepare both short- and long-range plans. They develop partnerships with power-connected people. They commit themselves to following through and they never give in to obstacles.

Today—take a look at where you are... and where you want to be. What are your priorities? How do you plan to get there? Remember, if you fail to plan—chances are you're planning to fail.

Make success a top priority.... It may demand a little extra effort, but if you want to win, you have to plan to win!

Make Libraries
and Bookstores
Your Best Friends

Zig Ziglar once said: "You can change what you are
by changing what goes into your mind."

Surviving and thriving in your career means
reading a little, every day...

Here's a lesson in getting ahead from Joel Weldon,
one of North America's most famous motivational
speakers:

"If you read just 12 pages per day," says Joel,
"you'll read over 17 books a year!"

If everyone did this, it would certainly change the
national average, which right now is only one book per
year. Reading for a few minutes each day can give you
an incredible edge—it can literally make you an expert
on almost any subject.

Make libraries and bookstores your best friends, and
you'll outsmart the competition.

Writing a Great
Letter of Application

*Writing a great cover letter
is the hardest part of applying for a job.*

*Surviving and thriving in your career means
captivating your audience...*

It never ceases to amaze me what little effort people invest in preparing a letter of application for a new job. A good letter has four parts:

1. An opening statement introducing the one aspect of your qualifications that will most interest your reader.

2. An outline of the key benefits you can provide the company.

3. A summary of how your skills, education, and personality match the requirements of the position.

4. An upbeat, enthusiastic ending, including a suggestion as to when the reader can expect a follow-up call from you.

Always take the time to prepare a cover letter that showcases the best of what you have to offer. Follow this formula, and you'll increase your chances of getting an interview.

Promote Yourself with a Living Résumé

*Do you want to wow potential employers
and create great opportunities for yourself?*

*Surviving and thriving on the job means
building a living résumé...*

A personal scrapbook, or "Living Résumé" as I call it, is one of the most powerful tools I use to promote myself. It attracts attention and literally captures the imagination of my prospects.

Here's how you can build yours:

1. Go to an art supply store and buy an easel-style portfolio.

2. Collect samples of your work—like reports, memos, charts, presentations, diplomas—anything that you can think of!

3. Oh yes... it's a scrapbook, so hunt down some pictures and don't forget your glowing reference letters.

4. Arrange all the pieces in a pleasing way. If you need help, ask a friend.

Turn your résumé into a Living Résumé and you'll stand out and get more work as a result.

Invest Your
Spare Time Wisely

*Volunteering is a great way
to get valuable job experience.*

*Surviving and thriving in your career means
investing some spare time...*

E ven if you're engaged in full-time work, you may
still have some free time. Volunteering is a way of
giving your life some structure and gaining valuable
experience that can help you in your paying job. Many
organizations provide excellent training and experience
in sales, management, and leadership.

In return for your contribution, they'll give you an
opportunity to meet new people, and learn new skills.

Apart from the experience, listing volunteer work on your
résumé tells an employer that you have initiative and a
sense of community responsibility, two key qualities in a
good employee.

So put your free time to good use as a volunteer. Your
life will be richly rewarded if you do.

The Power of
a Genuine Smile

*Your smile is more than just an expression...
it's a powerful form of personal advertising.*

*Surviving and thriving in your career means
showing people that you're happy...*

During the past 15 years, I've trained literally hundreds of clients in personal marketing and selling techniques. And it never ceases to amaze me how people get so far in life without being taught the tremendous value of a genuine smile.

George, one of my first bosses back in the late '70s, used to preach this constantly when he was teaching me how to run my first company. "Steve," he'd say, "when you walk into the office, the first thing your people are going to look at is your face. They're going to notice whether you're happy or not, whether you're motivated or not, whether you're stressed or not, all from what's happening between your two ears."

Your smile can be one of your biggest assets. So try one on, today!

Shaking Your Way to the Top

Your skill in meeting and greeting people is an important part of building a personal network.

Surviving and thriving in your career means shaking hands to get ahead...

When you're meeting people for the first time, how you shake hands is a big part of the impression you make. It's your way of making a personal connection with someone, especially someone you don't know. Here are some tips:

1. Present your hand fully, not just the fingertips.

2. Smile, look the person in the eye, shake twice, then release. Grip firmly, but don't squeeze any harder than the other person is squeezing. Just a hint—you shouldn't hear a crunch!

3. Like anything else, the key to a successful handshake is to feel good about it, feel like you really mean it.

Make your handshake your personal signature. You'll shake your way to the top if you do.

Turn Co-Workers
Into Cheerleaders

*A happy teammate can be your best ally
in your battle to stay ahead.*

*Surviving and thriving in your career means
turning your co-workers into cheerleaders...*

We all know about the value of word-of-mouth advertising to a business. But when you think about it, your co-workers can spread the good word about you and do more for your career than all of your efforts put together. Think about it: if a supervisor in another department recommends you for a promotion, your boss will likely pay attention. So, how can you get people selling you?

1. Impress them beyond their expectations by doing it faster and better.

2. Work hard to improve your efforts every day.

3. Always be enthusiastic about what you do and who you do it for.

Turn your co-workers into cheerleaders. Your career will take off if you do.

Staying Out of the Résumé Trashcan

In today's job market, it's vital that your résumé find its way into the right hands.

Surviving and thriving in your career means keeping your résumé out of the trashcan...

I learned an important lesson from Terry, one of the top program directors in Canadian radio.

Terry told me he gets dozens of applications from people looking for work at his station... and he's amazed by the number of job hunters who don't take the time to find out the correct spelling of his name, title, and address.

His screening technique certainly got my attention. He throws out all letters that aren't specifically addressed to him as well as all letters that misspell his name and title. He also pitches out those faxed from other radio stations!

If you do your homework, your properly addressed application will rise to the top of the pile.

Life's a Pitch!!

*Don Peppers, the New York adman,
is famous for his book* **Life's a Pitch.**

*Surviving and thriving in your career means
selling yourself 24 hours a day...*

My sister Leslie, who runs a travel business specializing in cruise vacations, recently took a cruise herself. At the dinner table on the ship she met three couples who asked her what she did for a living. She told them she ran a travel agency and gave them her business card.

When she got back, she received calls from each of the couples enquiring about other holidays, and by last week she had booked new trips for two of them. Leslie had turned "casual holiday contacts" into clients because she had had the foresight to take some business cards with her and promote her business on her holiday.

Be prepared to sell yourself 365 days a year. You just never know when a new client will come along.

Getting Your Calls Returned

*Do you deal with people who just
never return your telephone calls?*

*Surviving and thriving in your career means
getting people's attention...*

Despite all the advances in technology—voice mail, e-mail, cell phones, and satellite paging systems—it's getting harder and harder to reach someone on the phone, especially someone you don't know.

Chris, an Edmonton writer and entrepreneur, has come up with the perfect solution to this problem. He and his company have developed a neat line of greeting cards which he markets to people who want to introduce themselves in a unique way and make a great impression on a new client.

If you're having trouble getting your call returned, try sending a greeting card first.

Be with People Who Love to Win

Yachting champion Dennis Connor once said, "The secret is to surround yourself with quality crew members who just hate to lose."

Surviving and thriving in your career means being with people who love to win...

I read a great story about General William Westmoreland, the famous U.S. army commander in the Vietnam War.

Apparently, the general was reviewing a platoon of his best paratroopers one day. As he went down the line, he asked each of his troops the question: "How do you like jumping, son?"

"I just love it, sir!" was the first answer the general heard. "The greatest experience in my life, sir!" exclaimed a second paratrooper. But the third trooper said "I hate it, sir! But I do it because I want to be with the guys who love to jump."

People like being around winners, especially if they enjoy what they're doing.

Leave Your Mark
with a Bookmark

Do you want to stand out in the employment crowd and make a lasting impression?

Surviving and thriving on the job means creating a bookmark résumé...

One of my résumés is a bookmark. I've found that this 2" x 8" card is a very popular sales tool and conversation piece. Because it's unusual, clients keep it longer and don't tend to "file" it the way they do other résumés. My bookmark contains:

1. A brief outline of my business career.

2. Volunteer activities, professional associations.

3. Testimonials.

4. A small picture of myself.

5. My company logo and telephone number. The best part... it works!

Be creative and use a bookmark to help people remember you. You'll leave your mark if you do.

The Reason
Angels Can Fly

There's a wonderful saying: "Angels can fly because they take themselves lightly."

Surviving and thriving in your career means always having a great sense of humour...

H umour is a wonderful skill in helping us success- fully manage our lives. When I used to fix sick companies, I often told my employees, "The situation sure is hopeless, but it's definitely not serious!"

A well-delivered line cuts through all the stress and pressure in today's workplace with laser-like precision. A clever joke almost always puts life into perspective.

When we lose our ability to laugh, especially at our- selves, it doesn't take long before we become "uptight" and our performance starts to suffer.

Plan each day to bring a joke or funny story into the office. Laugh a little... you'll enjoy your job more and perform better if you do.

Working a Room

*Your ability to "work a room" is critical
if you want to build a successful network.
Surviving and thriving in your career means
knowing how to meet and greet...*

Patricia Nichol, author of the book, *The Power of
Positive Linking*, has some great suggestions for
those who want to improve their mingling skills:

1. Don't wait for people to come to you—introduce
   yourself.

2. Memorize a friendly, believable 15-second commer-
   cial about what you do for a living.

3. Carry enough business cards to give one to everyone
   you meet.

4. Make notes on the business cards you collect immediately after leaving so that you'll remember the
   contacts later.

Networking isn't just about meeting people, it's about
building relationships for the future.

Meetings that Matter

Your performance at interviews is all-important.

Surviving and thriving on the job means presenting yourself with panache...

Your performance during a job interview is often the measure of your success. What are the three most common mistakes people make during interviews?

1. **Candidates fail to prepare.** They forget that an interview requires as much preparation (and practice) as a major presentation for an important customer.

2. **People talk too much.** All too often they get carried away with meaningless chat and forget to get to the point as quickly as possible.

3. **They don't promote their strengths, their skills, and their achievements enough.** Many people neglect to specifically focus the discussion on how they can handle the job better than anyone else.

So get prepared, get focussed, and get organized to make the most of every interview. You'll get the job if you do.

How to Impress
Someone You Don't Know

*What's the easiest, most inexpensive way to impress
someone you don't know?*

*Surviving and thriving in your career means
making people feel special...*

Anyone in the sales business will tell you the sweet-est sound to a person's ear (and ego) is the sound of their name.

A couple of years ago, I met the president of a very successful company who made it a practice to learn the first names of each of the 750 people working for him. Can you believe it? Every week, he took an hour to memorize the names of new employees by studying pictures in their personnel files.

Imagine how employees, both new and old, must have felt when he walked through the factory and struck up conversations starting with their first name.

You stand out in the workworld by making a special effort to show a genuine and personal interest in other people.

Know Thy Enemy

There's a famous saying:
"Ignorance isn't bliss—it's oblivion."

Surviving and thriving in your career means
knowing your competitors inside out...

Everyone's been to Wal-Mart. But most people don't realize how Sam Walton built this billion dollar business. He spent hours studying his competition and copying the best of their ideas.

Sam did the research himself. In the early '50s, after hearing about a new concept in retailing called self-service, he took a bus from Arkansas to Minnesota to visit two stores where it was being tested. Armed with a tape recorder, Walton also frequently "walked the aisles" at Kmart stores, interviewing their employees and dictating notes about their prices.

Take the time to gather some intelligence on your competitors. You'll win the war if you do.

Look, Think, and Act Like a Winner

*To be successful in life you have to
think and act like a winner.*

*Surviving and thriving in your career means
paying attention to the details...*

Notre Dame Coach Lou Holtz once asked his team to dress smartly in shirt and tie for the bus ride to a road game at Purdue. He said: "If you're going to be a winner, you have to look like a winner!"

When the team arrived at the stadium, the coach remained silent, looked over the players, straightened a tie or two—and then proudly summoned the driver to open the bus door. His message was clear and his team went on to win!

While we're often reminded not to sweat the small stuff, don't ever take it for granted. You have to do those little things to score big!

Next time you want to win the game, you have to look and act the part. It's a winning combination!

"Thy Word is Thy Bond"

*Do you consistently follow
the first golden rule of customer service?*

*Surviving and thriving in your career means
remembering Thy Word is Thy Bond...*

Last week, I ordered some film from a service bureau. I called the day the order was to be delivered, and was told it wasn't ready because of "equipment problems." The next day it still wasn't ready... this time the excuse was that "other jobs were more important." Well, three days (and two broken promises) later I'm looking for a new supplier.

Whenever you make a promise to someone, whether it's a customer, a fellow employee or even your boss, you've got to follow through and do everything you can to make that commitment happen. If you can't, you've got to make absolutely sure that you keep the next promise, and that you show you care by inventing some creative way to "make up" for your missed commitment.

"Thy word is thy bond." If you say it, do it.

Two Minutes to Shine

*There's one question you're bound to hear
in a job interview.*

*Surviving and thriving in your career
means knowing how to
tell me a little bit about yourself...*

When you hear the most commonly asked job interview question: "So, tell me a little bit about yourself," are you ready to answer?

Your answer should be about two minutes long, and should showcase the best you have to offer. Start with a brief introduction, like your current employment situation or your recent school history.

Mention your key strengths and the achievements that demonstrate them. Relate these strengths to the needs of your prospective employer. Be as specific as you can.

Practice before each interview. Know what you want to say before you have to say it.

You won't know all the questions they're going to ask in an interview, but you can be well-prepared for this important one.

Never Forget
the Law of 250

*Word-of-mouth advertising can either
make or break a business or a career.*

*Surviving and thriving in your career means
never forgetting the Law of 250...*

Regardless of who you are or what you do for a living, if you want to be really successful in your career you have to remember that everything you do and say at work is important.

A long time ago I learned the Law of 250 from a friend who was a funeral director. He told me when ordering memorial cards to use at a funeral, 250 people was the average number of people that most of us know.

I started to think about that... 250 people.... That means when I do a good job for one person, they can potentially mention it to 250 people. Conversely, if I do a bad job, 250 people will know.

Remember, when you're honest, enthusiastic, and give your best effort, you automatically turn dozens of people into cheerleaders for your future success.

Dress to Impress

*There's a right and a wrong way
to dress for every occasion.*

*Surviving and thriving in your career means
dressing to impress...*

L ast week, I interviewed a candidate for a receptionist
position in our office. When she walked in the front
door, she was wearing a baggy sweater and track pants.
Before I'd even talked to her I'd already decided that she
wasn't suitable for the job. Her clothing totally destroyed
the impression created by her impressive résumé....

Think carefully about how you dress, wherever you are going.

1. It's a good idea to call first and ask how staff at your
   destination usually dress.

2. Your clothes should be clean, neatly pressed, and
   appropriate for your position.

3. Wear something that makes you feel good about
   yourself.

The right clothes will put you and those who meet you
at ease and set the stage for your success.

The Art of
Voice Management

Your voice is the sound of your soul.

Surviving and thriving in your career means turning your voice into a personal selling tool...

When you think about it, your voice can be one of your most attractive personal assets. The key to having a voice that people enjoy is to "vary the dynamics" of how fast you talk, how loudly you talk, and the pitch of your voice.

Here's how you can become more persuasive:

1. **Lower your pitch one or two tones.** Do this especially when you're making key points.

2. **Practice your articulation.** The best way to do this is by reading aloud. Try Dr. Seuss's *Cat in the Hat*.

3. **Raise those cheek muscles and smile!** It will help you articulate better.

Master the art of voice management. You'll win more friends and influence more people if you do.

Share Your Victories

*Do you spread the word
when you enjoy success at work?*

*Surviving and thriving in your career means
posting good news notes...*

A friend of mine recently found a way to save $150,000 for his company. I asked him, "Have you told anyone else besides your boss?" Can you believe it, he hadn't mentioned it to anyone. He'd missed a golden opportunity to share his victory with his teammates.

I once landed a huge order after chasing it for more than four months. Boy, was I excited! I immediately wrote a note announcing the sale and thanking everyone who helped me. I put a copy on each desk in the office, so the first thing everyone saw on Monday morning was a "good news note." We all enjoyed a great start to the week.

If you share your victories with your workmates, they'll appreciate you more and you'll give them a much-needed lift.

The Golden Rules
for Working

There's a famous saying...
"Actions speak louder than words."

Surviving and thriving in your career means
following the Golden Rules for Working...

A few years ago, I took a leadership course taught by one of Canada's foremost business professors. Not only did he teach me a lot about leadership, he also gave me some advice on working that I've followed religiously in my career....

The Golden Rules for Working

If it ain't broke, don't fix it.
If you break it, admit it.
If you value it, take care of it.
If you make a mess, clean it up.
If it belongs to someone else and you want to use it,
  get permission.
If it's none of your business, don't ask questions.
If it will tarnish someone's reputation, keep it to yourself.
If it will brighten someone's day, say it.

So remember this lesson on leadership... actions speak louder than words.

Add a "Personal Signature" to Your Work

Martin Luther King once said: "If a man is a street sweeper, he should sweep like Michelangelo."

Surviving and thriving in your career means adopting a personal signature...

I once spoke to a group of accountants on building customer loyalty and employee morale in the workplace.

I stressed the importance of adding a "personal signature" to your work. One of the most powerful ways to do this is to do something really different... something that's fun and makes you stand out.

I told the story of a travel agent I know who sends her cruise clients a giant, "thank you" cookie after they return from their vacations and a copywriter friend who always encloses a truffle with every invoice he gives his clients. Guess what? He always gets paid on time!

Get those creative juices flowing and come up with your own "personal signature." You'll build goodwill with your customers and feel better about your job if you do.

Treat Your References
with Respect

*There's a right and a wrong way
to use a reference for a job application.*

*Surviving and thriving in your career means
treating your references with respect...*

A former employee of mine recently gave my name as a reference without letting me know first. When I heard from her prospective employer, the call caught me totally off guard. I knew nothing about the job so I was unable to really help her.

1. You should always ask permission to use someone as a reference. Phone them first and tell them about the job.

2. Try to let them know when they can expect a call.

3. If you're successful, don't forget to send a thank-you note.

Treat your references with courtesy and respect. If you do, they'll be there when you really need them.

How to Get People to Like You

*Psychologist William James once wrote:
"One of the deepest drives of human nature
is to be sought after and appreciated."*

*Surviving and thriving in your career means
getting people to like you...*

L et's face it, all of us want to be popular, both at
work and at home.

The problem is, if you try too hard, chances are you'll
never be popular. However, there are some things you
can do to make yourself more likeable. For example:

1. Try to be easy-going, relaxed, and natural, someone
   who people can talk to.

2. Go out of your way to show that you enjoy being
   with people.

3. Focus only on the positive traits of the people you
   spend time with.

4. Make a habit of complimenting those who are
   important to you.

People who make an effort to be liked are much more
likely to succeed and get where they want to go.

Lessons from "The Art of War"

Sun Zsu, a Chinese warlord, wrote:
"Battles are won or lost before they are fought."

Surviving and thriving in your career means
planning to win the war...

People often ask me: "What are the most important factors in an individual's success?"

Well, success (or failure) is usually determined by two things: luck... and planning. Since we can't do much about luck, we have to plan... that is, we have to prepare a strategic personal marketing plan.

You see, marketing is very much like a game of chess. The player who moves without thinking will waste moves, lose pieces, and will probably lose the game. But the one who always analyses the opposition, continually assesses his or her position, and has a carefully thought-out plan for the next three to five moves, is the one who usually wins.

Take the time to "plan your attack." You'll "win the war" if you do.

Talk to People

You've heard of the big TV networks.
But how big is your personal network?

Surviving and thriving in your career means
making personal connections...

A successful friend of mine had just completed a big year. Everything was perfect. I asked her to reveal her secret: "Well, it's a networking game called TTP!"

She said: "TTP means Talk To People. It's as simple as that... talk to people and if you're still not meeting your goals TTMP... Talk to More People."

It's called *networking*, and could be your secret to success. Shake those hands, distribute those business cards. It's the perfect way to stay in the sunshine. After all... that's where the flowers grow!

Everyone is in the "people business".... Make those people connections... network! You have to stay in touch to be in touch.

Extraordinary, "Non-ordinary" Business Cards

Your business card makes a powerful statement.

Surviving and thriving in your career means having an extraordinary, non-ordinary business card...

Baron Hanson, head of The Extraordinary Business Card Company in Charlotte, North Carolina, thinks that every entrepreneur should spend a little extra money to create a really great business card. Why?

1. **A card is a reflection of you.** A great one shows you've taken the time to market yourself.

2. **It's a sample of the kind of work your company produces.** Great card, great work. Ordinary card, ordinary work.

3. **Also, it's the most potent form of lasting advertising.** Not every card you give away results in a sale. But if your card is great, people will keep it around until it's finally used.

You're giving your card to people who make critical decisions. The right card... the right decision.

Goin' the Extra Mile
for that New Job

*Smart job hunters today use
unconventional techniques to get interviews.*

*Surviving and thriving in your career means
goin' the extra mile...*

Paul, a 28 year-old friend of mine, works part-time at three different jobs. The other day he saw an ad for a great full-time position.

He called me... "Steve," he said, "I've sent in my résumé... but what else can I do to get on the short list? I really want this job!"

How about getting your five best reference letters together and sending them to the recruiter, along with a note saying how much you are interested in the position? Better still, put together a special "something" showcasing your talent and deliver it in person.

You've got to go the extra mile and pull out all the stops if you want to win the job search game.

How to Prepare An Irresistible Sales Brochure

*Do you want to impress new clients
the next time you make a sales call?*

*Surviving and thriving in your career means
handing out irresistible sales brochures...*

I f you blend the following ingredients, you'll serve up a tasty brochure for your prospects:

1. Start with a "hook" or headline that gets your client salivating.

2. Add a brief life sketch that showcases your unique offering, and season it with a warm, friendly photograph.

3. Mix in your selling script or pitch, highlighting the three to six reasons why clients should buy from you.

4. Sprinkle two or three testimonials throughout to add credibility.

5. Present it in an attractive, inviting way to whet the client's appetite for your service.

Remember these special ingredients the next time you cook up a new sales brochure. You'll delight your customers if you do.

part
TWO

How to Improve Your Performance on the Job

There is only one way to excel in your career, and that's by being better than your competitors. Whether you are an employee or an entrepreneur, success comes with self-improvement.

There is no way around the need to constantly challenge yourself to become a better person, to acquire new skills, to conquer old fears. When you are in competition, you can never rest on your laurels. You need to know how to measure yourself relative to your competitors, and then outdo them by improving yourself.

These tips all represent ways in which you can step above your rivals by making conscious attempts to better yourself and improve your performance. In making the effort, you will be assured of moving onward and upward, instead of staying put and being left behind.

Turn Voice Mail
into Action Mail

A dynamic voice mail message can be one of the most effective ways to communicate.

Surviving and thriving in your career means turning voice mail into action mail...

The key to leaving a dynamic voice mail message is being prepared. Your goal is to make each voice mail message an event... and a pleasure for your listener to review.

1. Before you start, jot down four or five key points as an outline of what you want to say, then mentally rehearse your message.

2. Introduce your call as you would a business letter, explaining who you are and why you're calling.

3. Keep your message friendly, brief, clear, and conversational.

4. Close with a distinctive, upbeat phrase that includes an invitation, like "Ciao for now, I hope to hear from you after 3 pm today!"

Voice mail doesn't have to be a barrier to getting things done. Use it correctly and you'll stand out and get ahead.

How to Make Successful Sales Calls

Organization is the secret
to every successful sales call.

Surviving and thriving in your career means
making persuasive sales pitches…

When you think about it, a succesful sales presentation depends not only on what you say but how you say it. Voice quality, body language, and appearance all create a total impression when you're selling yourself.

Choose your words carefully. Avoid words like "costly," "problem," or "difficult"… they trigger negative reactions in people.

Communicate clearly how you will meet your prospect's needs, not yours.

Finally, make sure you "engage your brain" before you answer any questions.

You're always selling yourself. Get organized, communicate clearly, and your pitch will be persuasive.

Without Data,
You're Just Another Opinion

Used correctly, facts and figures are an extremely effective way to sell your ideas.

Surviving and thriving in your career means being more than just an opinion...

Over the past ten years I've sold millions of dollars of products to one of Canada's largest companies. I can still remember the first presentation I made to their purchasing manager.... Boy, was I prepared! I spent hours creating fancy overheads, and I even practised my "sales pitch" in front of the mirror!

After all this extra effort, I didn't get the order. When I asked him why, he said, "Steve, your presentation said a lot, but didn't tell me anything. You didn't follow the cardinal rule of personal selling: **Without data, you're just another opinion.**"

The next time you're preparing a presentation, writing a report or just answering a question in a meeting, prove your case with numbers and facts.

Thank-you Notes
Are Like Diamonds

Surprise letters of appreciation
are a great tool to cement relationships.

Surviving and thriving in your career means
taking the time to say thank you...

Recently, I decided to try a new car wash business just around the corner from my office.

The owner showed his enthusiasm and interest in me as a long-term client right from the moment I arrived. He did a fabulous job on my vehicle but what made him stand out was the letter he left on my front seat.

"Dear Steve," he wrote, "I would like to thank you for choosing us to maintain your vehicle.... We trust you will be 100% satisfied, and please come back often to use our service.... Again, thank you."

This letter made me feel appreciated... like he really cared about his customers and about me, in particular.

An old-fashioned thank-you note is a great way to make a positive impression. Write them and you'll make new friends and earn more business.

Overcoming
Speech Fright

*Knowing how to deliver a speech effectively
is a critical success skill.*

*Surviving and thriving in your career means
overcoming speech fright...*

It's a common nightmare: being asked to stand up in front of an audience to make a presentation. Especially if the talk's about something really important, or if it's in front of people who are really important.

The secret to a great speech is practice. Know your material and have the confidence to say exactly what you want to say, when you want to say it. I rehearse a presentation in front of a mirror at least four or five times.

Another key is organization—preparing an outline of the talk from beginning to end.

A good speech also starts by getting the audience's attention and tells them what's in it for them if they keep listening.

Like any fearful situation, giving a speech gets easier if you practice and prepare.

"People First" Planning

*Do you and your colleagues want to give
your company a competitive edge?*

*Surviving and thriving in your career means
using "People First" Planning...*

Everyone in business knows they've got to plan to get ahead.... Involving all your co-workers in your plans is the key to success. I call this "People First" planning.

1. Before starting your plan, ask your colleagues and teammates for their input and opinions.

2. Ensure that your colleagues are given everything they need to work as team toward achieving common goals.

3. Develop a "culture" that builds commitment to your company's goals and rewards people for achieving them.

Whether your goals are big or small, getting your colleagues involved in your planning will give you an edge and get you where you want to go.

Turn Your E-Mail Address into a Marketing Tool

A "customer-friendly" e-mail address can be a fabulous way of promoting yourself.

Surviving and thriving in your career means turning your e-mail address into a marketing tool...

There's a lot you can do to make people remember you on the information super highway.

With the help of my Internet provider, I developed a memorable e-mail address (steve@marketingbreakthroughs.com) that many of my clients have complimented me on. Here's the formula:

1. Use your first name to start the address, the one most people know you by.

2. Ask your provider if you can use your company name immediately after the "@" symbol.

3. Try to keep numbers out of your address.

4. Make sure you display your address in all your personal advertising, like on business cards, faxes, and memos.

An easy-to-use, easy-to-remember e-mail address will put a smile on your customers' faces, every time they send you a message!

"Hi, Bill,
Nice to Meet You!"

Author Peter Legge once wrote:
"It's our name that gives each of us a special identity."

Surviving and thriving in your career means
saying the magic word...

Bill Clennan calls himself Mr. Memory. Up to 250 times a year, he speaks to audiences around the world about his memory techniques and the importance of remembering people's names.

Bill teaches that you make people feel good by mentioning their names frequently during a conversation. It's as simple as starting a sentence with a person's name. "Bill, I'd like you to meet Barbara." "Hi, Barbara, nice to meet you."

You win friends and make long-lasting impressions by using people's names when you're talking to them.

Everybody Needs
Good News

Everybody needs a generous helping of good news.
It's the garden where optimism grows!

Surviving and thriving in your career means
being a good news giver...

Before you spread some doom and gloom—shout some "good news" around, share it, and create positive energy with everybody.

If the sales force has made some great sales, let people know. If a fellow colleague has been promoted, let people know. If you've been able to solve a problem, let people know. And even if you've made a mistake and have rectified it, let people know.

Imagine the impact you'll make on your boss, your colleagues, and your friends and family when you bring home the good news. It may be a welcome change!

Spread some good news around today... see the smiles and enjoy the moment! Everyone around you will appreciate it.

Being "Letter Perfect"

*Your writing skills send a
powerful message about who you are.*

*Surviving and thriving in your career means
sending out work that's letter perfect every time...*

I once received a letter from a vice-president of one of
Canada's most respected companies. I couldn't
believe this letter! Three grammar mistakes, two
spelling mistakes, and the print was so small I needed a
magnifying glass to read it!

These days, the appearance, construction, and quality of
a letter still say a lot about who's writing it. Here's some
advice:

1. Use 14-point type. It will make your sentences stand
    out and much easier to read.

2. Keep your paragraphs brief.

3. Personally check, and then double check, to make
    sure all the words are spelled perfectly.

Take the time to make sure your letters are shining
examples of English 101. You'll sell your ideas and
impress people if you do.

Stick to Your Customers—Like Glue

Building a lasting relationship with a client is one of the toughest things to do in business.

Surviving and thriving in your career means sticking to your customers—like glue…

Last week, I asked one of Canada's top new car salesmen about his formula for building successful, long-term relationships with clients.

"Steve," he said, "I constantly remind customers I'm there to help them."

"First, I send a handwritten note thanking customers for their business, mailed within hours after their car is delivered.

"Next, I send a second letter, one month later, making sure they're 100% satisfied with their purchase and offering to help if they're not.

"Finally, I send another note, three months later, telling them that I'm always available to assist them, day or night."

Whether you're selling a car or even yourself, it's what you do after you've made the sale that helps you "bond" with your customers.

Make Friends
With Your Customers

We all know how friendships grow,
but how about business careers?

Surviving and thriving in your career means
making friends with your customers...

A recent survey by PROFIT magazine found that successful entrepreneurs follow a special formula for growing their companies:

1. They make doing business with them a pleasure. They pay attention to detail and keep in touch with customers. They reward employees for outstanding customer service.

2. They learn about their clients and constantly update their database.

3. They always give customers something extra, like gifts or special offers.

You have to "make friends" with your customers if you want to build a prosperous business career.

The Warm and Friendly Follow-up

A hand-delivered follow-up letter is a powerful way to make a lasting personal impression.

Surviving and thriving in your career means following up to get ahead...

Whenever you make a first time sales presentation or job interview you should always follow up with a letter, to remind the customer of the highlights of the meeting. Keep the letter warm and friendly.

1. Thank the person for the opportunity.

2. Remind him or her of the benefits you offer and why you should be considered for the order.

3. Summarize the next steps in the process as you understand them.

4. Indicate what your next action will be. For example, "I'll call you next week..."

A great touch is to hand deliver your letter if possible. Never fax it. If you must mail it, send it by courier.

So, write a warm, friendly follow-up letter after your next sales call. It will help you stand out if you do.

Making Change
Work For You

*Are you responsible for planning
a major change at work?*

*Surviving and thriving in your career means
successfully introducing change...*

If you're in charge of planning a major change in
your company, you'll have a better chance of suc-
ceeding if you remember some basics:

1. Get people at all levels involved right from the beginning. This gives them input and a chance to prepare.

2. Introduce the change gradually. Allow people time
   to adjust and integrate the change into their existing
   routines.

3. Finally, if you're changing a system or procedure,
   have a backup plan in case the new system doesn't
   work out.

Remember, plan your changes carefully before you
start. You'll make change work for you if you do.

E-Mail Etiquette

*Electronic mail can either be a blessing
or a curse for those of us who are wired.*

*Surviving and thriving in your career means
following e-mail etiquette...*

Nathalie, a friend of mine, called me about a really
rude and nasty e-mail message she'd received
from one of her co-workers. She told me that many people in her company need a lesson on e-mail etiquette:

1. Don't send an e-mail when you could just as easily
   deliver the message personally, or on the telephone.

2. Never use it to "report" about another person's
   performance.

3. Don't use it for confidential messages. If walls have
   ears, networks certainly have eyes!

Writing an e-mail memo is just another way of writing
a conventional memo—follow the same rules and you'll
be more successful.

The More You Plant, the Greater Your Harvest

*Networking is a powerful way
to generate new clients for your business.*

*Surviving and thriving in your career means
building a bigger and better network...*

If there's one thing I've learned over the years, it's the more people I know, the bigger my network and the more business I have.

Set a goal to distribute business cards to at least five new people each week. And, since you always give two cards to each person, you have the potential of reaching ten new prospects, that's 520 a year!

Also, think of an intriguing answer to the popular party question, "So, what kind of work do you do?" When I ran a turnaround consulting company my answer was "I fix sick companies." It always led to more conversation and an opportunity to plant a few seeds.

Networks are like gardens, the more contacts you plant, the greater your career harvest.

Putting Your
Walls to Work

*Do your office walls help
promote you in your career?*

*Surviving and thriving in your career means
putting your walls to work...*

When clients come into our office, their eyes always move immediately to our "brag wall," and while they're waiting, they read the framed letters and look at the pictures that hang there. These momentos are effective sales aids and conversation pieces and they create a warm, positive impression about our business.

Collect letters that recognize your talents and achievements. Also, use photos (especially ones depicting happy customers) and don't forget community service plaques and certificates. Choose the best, frame them, and put them where clients and colleagues can see them.

Use your walls to sing your praises. It will be music to your visitors' ears.

Even Great Ideas
Need to Be Sold

Do you have a great idea to help your company but don't know how to sell it to your boss?

Surviving and thriving in your career means delivering a winning sales pitch...

Okay, you have a great idea to cut expenses or improve sales, and you want to sell the idea to management, but you're not quite sure how to do it. Here are some tips:

1. Prepare a 500-word explanation of the idea and a carefully researched outline of its costs and benefits.

2. Ask a colleague to help you fine-tune this summary.

3. Then, ask your boss for a meeting so that you can present it in person.

4. Finally, make sure you get a commitment on what your boss is planning to do with your suggestion.

Even great ideas need to be pitched before they are implemented. Sell them effectively and you'll get ahead.

If You Don't Ask ...

It's amazing how you can get ahead just by asking.

Surviving and thriving in your career means getting what you want...

Six years ago a budding entrepreneur asked 35 CEOs of big companies for advice on setting up a software business. Fifteen agreed to help. Three of those people now sit on the board of his 21 million dollar company.

Now, you don't have to always ask 35 CEOs for help. Just recently I rented a portable sign to advertise one of my seminars. I asked the owner if he'd like to cross market with me. He said yes. So, I got a deal on the sign just by asking for it.

Next time you want something, why not just ask? You may be surprised by the result.

Everybody's in Sales

Everyone in your office should be a salesperson.

Surviving and thriving in your career means recruiting all your teammates to the sales force...

Every employee is a salesperson for your company. But you have to make sure they have the equipment to do the job.

Do all your teammates understand exactly what services the company offers or what products it makes? Can they explain what makes your company different from your competitors?

Employees should be familiar with the "big picture," not just their specific job. They should feel part of something bigger than their own department. And they should be proud to work for the company.

Reward and recognize your employees for bringing in new customers with incentive programs or special gifts.

If you turn your office into a company full of non-sales "sales people," you'll move up to the top.

Turn E-Mail into "Effective Mail"

*There's a right way and a wrong way
to compose e-mail.*

*Surviving and thriving in your career means
turning Electronic Mail into Effective Mail...*

Research shows that the average person working for
a big company sends and receives over 50 e-mail
messages a day! Yet very few of us have been trained in
this "new" method of communication.

Here's a really handy guide to help you prepare more
effective e-mail:

1. Reply as fast as you can to a message. Don't keep
   people waiting.

2. Keep your messages short and to the point.

3. Send "CCs" only to the people who really need them.

4. Insert as many headings as you can. This makes
   your copy more visually appealing.

5. Avoid capitalizing full words—it's considered rude
   and makes your message harder to read.

If you use this common-sense guide for e-mail, your
messages will be clear, concise, and more compelling.

If It's Easy to Read, It's Easy to Remember

Do you want your ideas to stand out the next time you write a proposal or letter?

Surviving and thriving in your career means inviting and enticing your readers...

With all the desktop publishing software on the market, it's becoming easier and easier to prepare proposals and letters. However, even with the best software, you still have to follow four rules to design a dynamite looking document:

1. Keep the margins 1" all around.

2. Justify the copy flush left, ragged-right.

3. Start a paragraph at least every four sentences.

4. Include two to four headlines on each page to dramatize and sharpen your message.

Make your proposals and letters easy and inviting to read. You'll treat your readers to a "memorable" reading experience if you do.

Overcoming the
New Job Jitters

*Your first few weeks in a new job
can be pretty tense.*

*Surviving and thriving in your career means
overcoming new job jitters...*

Congratulations! After looking for work you've found a job! How do you make the most of it?

Well, you wouldn't be human if you didn't feel anxious, but remember, *you* were hired. Tell yourself you deserve the job.

Next, write down all the personal qualities and skills you have to offer. Visualize yourself as the perfect employee.

Don't forget, ask for help when you need it, and set realistic goals for yourself. Take your time and get a feel for the office social scene and politics. Finally, be on the lookout for ways to impress both your boss and your teammates.

Remember, think positively about yourself and your new job. You'll make a lasting first impression if you do.

The "Red Carpet Telephone Treatment"

What's the first impression people get when they call your office?

Surviving and thriving in your career means starting off great from the hello...

A recent study found that 87% of CEO's formed their opinion of a business by how the phone was answered.

When people call you, what do they hear? Does your answering voice convey warmth and energy? Do they "hear" a smile?

Do all the people who answer the phone in your office use the same friendly opening? Are they brief and sincere, or do they sound memorized or automatic?

Try calling your own business and listen to how the phone is answered. Would you do business with your company?

Give your clients the red carpet telephone treatment. It's the most important personal advertising you'll ever do.

Boosting Sales Without Boosting Expenses

One of Canada's foremost marketing experts once taught me a valuable lesson.

Surviving and thriving in your career means boosting sales without boosting expenses...

One of my old marketing professors used to make the point: "It costs six times as much to get business from new customers than it does from old ones."

A few months ago a friend of mine who owns a wholesale coffee company started a marketing blitz. She called two former clients each day for 20 days. During these calls she re-introduced herself, and promoted her new line of flavoured coffees.

Her 40 calls produced 17 orders—an astonishing 42% closing rate!

Remember former customers the next time your business needs a quick sales boost. You'll be glad that you did.

Use the Magic of Press Releases

A well-written press release can win free publicity for you and your company.

Surviving and thriving in your career means using the media to get ahead...

Whenever you or your company do something out of the ordinary, make sure the media knows with a creative press release.

1. Pick an angle that will capture the interest of the reporter. Highlight the key elements that will have appeal for their audience.

2. Include a contact name and phone number and indicate the release date.

3. Type it double-spaced, and make sure it's completely free of errors.

4. Hand deliver it if possible. Don't fax it, it will get lost in "the pile." And always follow up with a telephone call the next day.

A well-written press release can get you great exposure at a price that's hard to beat.

Pink Slip Etiquette

*There's a right way and a wrong way to say
"You're fired."*

*Surviving and thriving in your career means
knowing how to hand out pink slips...*

I f you think about it, when a company lets somebody
go, you find out whether they really care about people.

Believe it or not, there is a firing etiquette—rules to follow
to keep the process as pain free as possible:

1. You should never fire someone on a Friday, or on
    their birthday or wedding anniversary.

2. Always do it in person, never by phone or e-mail.

3. Hold the meeting as early in the day as possible, and
    keep the interview brief and to the point, no more
    than 15 minutes.

Treat people like you'd want to be treated when you
hand out a pink slip. It's always in your best interest if
you do.

Sales Proposals
Made Easy

One of the secrets of being a successful salesperson is to master the art of proposal selling.

Surviving and thriving in your career means selling it in writing...

L et's face it, most of us approach the job of writing a sales proposal like we're about to get a tooth pulled. What people don't realize is that a well-written proposal can be a powerful force in convincing your customer to say "Yes!" to you and what you're selling.

The best proposals contain five key sections:

1. The introduction—a review of the specific customer needs.

2. Recommendations and your plan to help the customer.

3. An outline of the costs involved.

4. A summary of the benefits of doing business with you.

5. A call for action with a review of the next steps in the purchase.

Well-written sales proposals are like gold. Master the art of preparing them and you'll be richly rewarded.

Leading Through Change

If you're a leader at work,
you can help others deal with change.

Surviving and thriving in your career means
leading through change...

If you're a manger today, you need to remember three things:

1. **You need to speak in ways your workmates can understand, not in "leaderspeak."** You have to understand the emotions of those who are seeing their workmates lose their jobs and are worrying about their own jobs.

2. **You have to be comfortable not knowing all the answers.** Accept that things will often go wrong, and give them a chance to go right.

3. **You need to gain trust.** Be up front with employees and commit yourself to working out problems.

If you can transform change from a threat to a motivational challenge, you'll be more effective and get more done.

The Art of Imagining

Your imagination is a huge source of ideas to promote yourself and your career.

Surviving and thriving in your career means using cherry pies to get attention...

People love the unusual. One way to get somebody's attention is to send them an unusual gift. Advertising guru Jerry Goodis once had limousines deliver 25 corporate executives a cherry pie with a note saying "I bet you want a bigger slice of your market." He had very few turndowns when he called for an appointment.

For media exposure, try to think of a twist that makes what you are doing different from what everybody else is doing. Goodis once moved his office to his boat for the summer and told the local paper about it. He got a half page of free publicity.

Remember, you don't need a big budget to make an impact, just a little imagination and creativity.

Exceptional Employees = Exceptional Companies

Exceptional employees create exceptional companies.

Surviving and thriving in your career means making people feel good...

A survey of Canada's fastest-growing companies revealed one thing in common—they value their employees very highly and work hard to keep them happy and productive.

While money isn't the primary motivator for most people, half these companies pay higher than the average rate in their industry. All of them invest in training.

They take a personal interest in their people and offer benefits like Internet accounts or paid personal days off.

These companies expect a lot, but reward their employees with a pleasant workspace and fun social events.

Your employees are your most valuable asset. Treat them well and your business will thrive.

Appreciating Good Work

Successful managers always recognize their employees' achievements.

Surviving and thriving in your career means giving honest praise...

Every successful person I've met is successful because they recognize the efforts of their employees. Praise costs nothing, and it motivates.

To be effective, praise should be timely, sincere, and specific.

Choose a method that suits your personality and leadership style. Write notes to staff at the end of the day, stop by for a personal chat, or try beginning a staff meeting with testimonials from customers.

If you find it hard to give praise, keep one thought in mind: how good it feels when you're told you're doing a good job.

Let your employees know that you appreciate their good work. You'll be a much better manager if you do.

part
THREE

How to Use Career Self-Defense Moves to Stay Employed

I n these days of downsizing, you should be going to work with a selfish motive: protecting your income stream. You want to make sure your income is there for you next week, next month, next year.

The tips in this section are career self-defense moves you can use to avoid being downsized. They are not ways to play better office politics or being the "boss's pet." What matters most in the business world today is performance. If you aren't performing better than your competitors, you won't make the grade.

These scripts represent real-world strategies for protecting your income stream. Adopt them, and you can defend your career against uncertainty.

Career Mistake #1

When it comes to career opportunities,
the grass isn't always greener.

Surviving and thriving in your career means
knowing when to jump the fence...

Christine, a friend who's been a production manager in a really successful company for 12 years, called me for some advice. She had just received an offer to be general manager of another much smaller business and wasn't sure whether to accept it. I told her:

1. Look into the owner's financial background first.

2. Investigate the company's current bank financing.

3. Check out the management history of the company, including that of the previous general manager.

4. Make sure the owner has a crystal clear vision of where he/she wants the company to go.

Remember, check the company's background the next time you get a job offer. You could avoid making a BIG career mistake if you do.

What to Do After "Bad News from the Boss"

These days, getting a negative performance appraisal should send up a BIG, red flag.

Surviving and thriving in your career means paying attention to bad news from the boss...

A friend of mine just paid a terrible price for not paying attention to his "not so good" performance appraisal. After reading it, I suggested that he immediately start looking for a new job. "I've been here 18 years," he insisted, "they'll keep me on." Well, six weeks later he was fired!

If you receive "bad news from the boss," your self-defense antennae should instantly go up, way, way up. Normally, good bosses want to work with employees to correct their problems. If that isn't happening to you, it's probably because they don't expect you to be around much longer!

Don't think "it couldn't possibly happen to me"—these days it can happen to anyone.

Protect Yourself from Idea Thieves

*If you have a great business idea,
you have to protect it.*

*Surviving and thriving in your career means
avoiding intellectual theft...*

D on't make the mistake of giving away your ideas
without ensuring you'll get the credit you deserve.

If you have a great idea, think carefully before you present it. There is little to stop your boss, your partners, or your competitors from benefitting from your idea, unless you take steps to protect yourself.

Maintain a written "history" of your idea so you can point to hard "evidence" of your ownership. Keep a diary of your conversations with others.

You should always ask a potential partner to sign a confidentiality and non-competition agreement before you disclose your idea.

If your idea is a slogan or a symbol, apply for copyright or trademark protection.

Your ideas are valuable. You'll stay ahead of the pack only if you protect them.

Don't Forget Your
Office Party Etiquette

*Office "get-togethers" are often fun and can provide
great networking opportunities, but they also can
cause big problems.*

*Surviving and thriving in your career means
avoiding the career-ending office party...*

The other day I was talking to the receptionist of
one of my clients who was planning their Christ-
mas party. I said, "It looks like you're going to have a
good time." "I'm not sure I'm going," she said, "these
things always end up ruining somebody's career."

I told her, "You should reconsider... office parties are a
great way of getting to know people and, guess what, you
might even have some FUN!" Keep in mind though:

1. Watch your alcohol intake. If you want to "drink,"
   do it sparingly.

2. Stay with the people you want to be with.

3. Don't talk about the office or gossip about fellow
   employees.

Enjoy social occasions at your office, but don't forget
your etiquette. You'll continue to thrive in your career.

"Thanks Boss"

*Have you ever thought of sending your boss
a thank-you note?*

*Surviving and thriving in your career means
remembering your boss is human too...*

When your boss does something that helps you in your job, take the opportunity to express your appreciation with an old-fashioned thank-you note. Write the note on company letterhead, but make the letter personal and heartfelt, expressing your thanks for the specific help offered. Indicate how you felt about your boss's assistance or how it helped you to be more effective in your job.

A thank-you letter makes your boss feel good about how he or she is doing their job. It also shows that you care about the effort others make for you. In this age of cybercommunication, an old-fashioned thank-you note is still a mark of a true professional.

A written note of thanks for help from your boss is not only a great idea, it's also a wise career move.

Do Your Homework Before You Start Class

Choosing your next career training program requires brainwork and legwork.

Surviving and thriving in your career means doing your homework before you start class...

My nephew has just graduated from university and is planning his next career move. He wants to be a teacher and has applied to several teachers' colleges. I asked him if he knew what the job placement statistics were. Can you believe it? He didn't know.

Do your research before you start and invest in any career training course.

1. Get information about where the jobs will be in the next year and five years from now.

2. Ask about placement rates.

3. Talk to recent grads about their success in finding jobs.

Choose your next career training course with care. You'll make the right career move if you do.

Staying Happily Employed
Year After Year

*What's the secret to staying happily employed
year after year?*

*Surviving and thriving in your career means
making a difference...*

I remember visiting a Toronto radio station for the
first time a few months ago. I walked in and intro-
duced myself to Dianne, their receptionist for the past
18 years.

In spite of the many distractions and demands of her
job, Dianne made me feel right "at home." While sign-
ing courier slips, fielding a dozen different calls, and
handing out prizes, she treated me like I was the most
important person in her life at that time.

Just before we finished our conversation I asked her
what her secret was?

She thought for a minute, then finally said, "Well, I
really care about what I do... and I come to work each
day wanting to make a real difference."

Remember, you stay employed by making a difference.

Problems are
Windows of Opportunity

All problems are begging to be solved—
all they need are solutions!

Surviving and thriving in your career means
opening up to solutions...

One time I had a boss who blatantly pasted a notice
on his door: "Come in here only with solutions—
I already have problems!"

Far too many people march into the manager's office and
burden him or her with problem after problem. Some
bosses would faint if a solution were to enter the door!

Today, corporations everywhere are looking for people
who can systematically offer solutions to most problems. Solving problems brings a certain ray of sunshine
into the office and allows everyone to share in the hard-
fought victory!

Give your boss a gift! First thing tomorrow morning,
walk in with a solution—and you'll bring the sunshine in!

Set Up Your Career "Safety Deposit Box"

An important key to your future job security is the people you know.

Surviving and thriving in your career means setting up your career safety deposit box...

What's a career "safety deposit box"? Well, it serves the same purpose as your bank box, it just looks different. It's your Rolodex, or your business card file. You should be constantly adding names of new contacts and business associates. Set a goal to collect at least ten cards a week, from people that you know and meet—for example, fellow employees, suppliers, customers, even competitors.

If you need help in your present job, or with a future career move, the chances are pretty good you'll find that help from a person stored in your card file.

Make regular deposits to your career "safety deposit box." Some day soon, you'll be glad you did.

Dodging Those Downsizing Bullets

*More and more, it seems job security
is a thing of the past.*

*Surviving and thriving in your career means
dodging those downsizing bullets...*

Whether you're working for a big company or a small one, everyone needs a self-defense strategy to help dodge bullets from the "firing squad."

Here are some tips:

1. Make a date with yourself every month to assess your "bottom line" contribution to your employer.

2. Constantly look for opportunities to sharpen and acquire new skills.

3. Get in your boss's "good books" and develop an excellent rapport with the people you work for.

4. Always keep your ears open for rumours of impending cuts. More often than not, there's some truth to them.

In the new economy, successful people take steps to protect their jobs and improve their chances of surviving a downsizing.

Keep a
Personal Scrapbook

*Keeping a personal scrapbook
will pay big dividends in your career.*

*Surviving and thriving in your career means
building your file...*

Recently, a friend of mine came up with a fabulous idea to promote his employer. On his own time, he designed a new floor plan and layout to revamp the waiting area at the office. What a design! It was full of testimonials and pictures of happy customers—it even had mood music and incense.... The company loved it!

I asked him what he had "kept on file" as a visual record of this achievement. Any pictures of the new design? Or better still, any letters from his boss commenting on his talents?

Can you believe it—he'd spent over 60 hours on this project, yet he had nothing to show someone else what he'd accomplished.

Keep a visual record of your achievements. Someday soon, you'll be glad you did.

It's the Little Things that Count

Do you come to work each day actually planning to beat the competition?

Surviving and thriving in your career means doing the little things to be the best...

L ate last year, I spent an hour with the news director of a radio station in Ottawa.

During our conversation, he mentioned he'd been with the station for 20 years!

I asked him "What's your secret for career survival?" "Steve," he said, "I expect everyone here, especially myself, to take charge and take full responsibility for their jobs. That means not only do they have to write and deliver the news, they're going to do it better than the competition. They're going to come up with a special angle or edge every day to make sure that our product is better than everyone else's."

You get to the top (and stay there) only by outperforming the competition every day you're at work.

"Dig a Well
Before You're Thirsty"

*A famous Chinese proverb says
"Dig a well before you're thirsty."*

*Surviving and thriving in your career means
constantly preparing for change...*

Over the past few years I've learned that you have to prepare for change long before the actual change happens. And the people who manage change best are people who are constantly learning.

Think about the successful people you know. They are likely successful because they are continually learning and developing their competitive edge. They are ready for change because they are always sharpening their "edge" for the future.

Do you spend at least 10% of your time on self-improvement? Like going to night school, reading, or even going to conferences?

Change is constant in our lives. Make learning a constant, and you'll handle tomorrow's change just fine.

Act Like a "Free Agent"

Are you worried about losing your job?
Surviving and thriving in your career means
always improving your résumé...

According to management expert Tom Peters, the best approach to protecting your job today is to perform at work as if you're about to be laid off.

Peters says you have to think like you're a "free agent" preparing for your next assignment. You have to continually ask yourself questions like:

1. What do I really accomplish each day?

2. What have I done recently to help someone else?

3. Do I have customers who will give me a great reference?

4. What proof do I have that my skills are state of the art?

5. Will my year-end résumé look different than it did last year?

In the new economy, job security depends on you making your résumé noticeably better every three months.

Winning Your Boss's "Appraisal Game"

*Do you want to earn praise (and a big raise)
after your next performance review?*

*Surviving and thriving in your career means
winning your boss's appraisal game...*

Last week I had lunch with the advertising manager
of one of Canada's largest companies. Boy, was he
stressed! "Steve," he said, "I've got my annual review
next week... and I'm really worried."

I told him, the only way you're going to do well is to
prepare—prepare like you deserve loads of credit—like
you deserve a BIG raise.

1. Make a list of your top ten achievements. Be sure
   you've got accurate dates, facts, and figures.

2. Make a list of the top five things you've done to help
   your teammates and your boss.

3. Make a list of the top five things you're going to do
   to help your company make more money in the next
   six months.

If you prepare you'll score "big" the next time you play
your boss's appraisal game.

Are You Ready to be Downsized?

Everyone's heard the expression
"Always have a Plan B."

Surviving and thriving in your career means
being ready to be downsized...

Let's face it, every coach in professional sport is hired to be fired, and over the past few years, hundreds of thousands of workers in North America have been downsized—and this trend is predicted to continue.

I've coached dozens of people who've lost their jobs and I'm always amazed at how little prepared people are. Nobody ever has a "Plan B." You should:

1. Always have an up-to-date résumé and list of work references on file.

2. Always be on the lookout for better jobs with other companies.

3. Start a small home-based business in your spare time.

Re-engineering, re-structuring, re-everything is a constant in our lives. Have a "Plan B" and you'll handle tomorrow's surprises just fine.

Be a Winner,
Not a Whiner

*If you're complaining on the job,
you could be hurting your career.*

*Surviving and thriving in your career means
being a Winner not Whiner...*

While on vacation recently I listened to a friend's litany of complaints about her job. Nothing, it seemed, was right about the company, her colleagues, or her position. Wanting to be a good listener and not a critic, I didn't ask her the obvious question: "If it's so bad, why are you still working there?

If you can't fix it, live with it. If you can, do it. Being negative at work damages your morale and that of your workmates. A negative attitude can also lead to poor performance, cost you a promotion, and damage your relationship with colleagues.

No job is perfect, so stay positive about the one you have. You'll be a better employee if you do.

Bulletproofing Your Job

*Circulating copies of your work is a
really effective way to "bulletproof" your job.*

*Surviving and thriving in your career means
keeping your boss in the loop...*

I've worked for many bosses over the years, and if
there's one thing I've learned it is that you can never
assume anything—especially when you're working for
someone new.

The office copier and e-mail are great inventions, and
they can be your best allies in your quest to communicate and make your boss's life easier.

Copies show that you're doing what you're supposed to
be doing, when you're supposed to be doing it.

They ensure that your boss always knows what's going on.

And, they're also a great way to show your initiative,
creativity, and achievements on the job.

"CC" your work to keep your boss informed and "in
the loop." You'll leave nothing to chance and keep your
boss a lot happier if you do.

Get Rid of the "It's Not My Job" Syndrome

In the new economy, it only takes four words to destroy your career.

Surviving and thriving in your career means never ever saying "It's not my job!"...

With full-time jobs disappearing at an alarming rate, people just can't risk thinking, saying or even acting like "It's not my job." To protect your job today, you have to be willing to do everything you can to make your company a success—because if your company survives and thrives, it's likely that you will too.

To defend your career you need to be the kind of employee who solves problems, one who can "fill in" and do a variety of jobs. Somebody who can be counted on in a pinch, somebody who is eager for more responsibility.

Get rid of the "it's not my job" syndrome and you're far more likely to stay employed.

The Best Defense
Is a Good Offense

*In sports, we often hear the phrase
"the best defense is a good offense."*

*Surviving and thriving in your career means
preparing your personal career offense...*

Most of us work hard and make a contribution to
our company. Yet, many people don't take the time
to keep an accurate record of what they achieve on the job.

One of my first bosses taught me to keep a weekly job
diary. He called this my "personal career offense." Each
page included answers to the following three questions:

1. **What did you do to either make or save money
   this week?**

2. **What did you do to help your boss and your
   teammates?**

3. **What did you do to invest in your future?**

Remember, take 15 minutes each week to prepare your
own career offense—you'll find this diary really handy the
next time you're hunting for a raise or even a new job.

What to Do
if You Get the Ax

*Literally hundreds of people
are getting fired every day.*

*Surviving and thriving in your career means
knowing what to do if you're downsized...*

People often ask me: "What should I do if I get fired?"

Well, if you ever get the call into the boss's office:

1. Listen carefully and take notes during the discussion or immediately afterwards. Write down exactly what's said.

2. Don't commit to any offer or sign anything.

3. Don't get into a debate about why you're being fired, no matter how tempting.

4. Try to end the interview quickly, within five to ten minutes. Leave the building as soon as possible. Go home, calm down, and think about your options.

If you lose your job, don't lose your head. Use common sense and you'll be better off.

Get the Law on Getting Downsized

If you're downsized, you owe it to yourself to get good legal advice.

Surviving and thriving in your career means knowing who to talk to...

The first thing you should do if you're ever fired is discuss your situation with a specialist in employment law.

To find an employment lawyer, look in the Yellow Pages or ask your provincial law society to recommend someone.

Look for a lawyer who works primarily for employees, and don't be shy about asking how successful they've been in recent cases.

Also, ask if they offer a free half hour consultation. If the answer is no, go elsewhere.

When you meet, quiz them about their rates and find out how they're going to bill you.

If you're fired, get the best legal advice you can from a specialist. It's an investment you owe yourself.

Treat Your Boss
Like Your Best Customer

*What's the most important thing
you can do to protect your job?*

*Surviving and thriving in your career means
treating your boss like your best customer...*

I wish I had a nickel for all the people I've met who think of their boss the same way they think of income taxes and traffic jams.

I learned years ago that my boss held most of the keys to my career success. One of my first managers used to say, "Steve, I'm not your enemy—I'm your friend. I'm not your headache—I'm your job doctor. I'm not your warden—I'm your teacher. I'm not your obstacle course —I'm your opportunity. I'm not your boss—I'm your best customer."

In today's new economy, treating your boss like you want to be treated is more important than ever.

Checking the "Vital Signs" of Your Company

Do you really know whether your company is healthy and has a bright future?

Surviving and thriving in your career means giving your employer a check-up...

A couple of years ago, Eaton's shocked Canadians by filing for protection from its creditors. Ultimately, this venerable Canadian retailer closed its doors for good. With more and more stories like this, it's smart business to check the vital signs of your employer, every two or three months.

1. Watch for frequent calls from creditors, or rapid turnover in accounting or upper management.

2. Pay attention if consultant after consultant arrives to give top management fresh ideas on what they should be doing.

3. Finally, ask yourself: Are things improving? Are sales going up? Is your company really beating the competition?

Remember, to defend your career succesfully it's absolutely essential that you monitor your company's health.

Leaving a Positive Final Impression

How you leave a job is just as important as how you start it.

Surviving and thriving in your career means creating a positive final impression...

Excellent references are an essential part of any career self-defense strategy. One way to get a good reference is to follow four rules when you resign:

1. Give more notice than is required by law or company policy. If it's two weeks, give them three.

2. Maintain your work habits and commitment to the job right to the last day.

3. Update your files and tie up any loose ends you can.

4. Make sure other staff know what's left to be done. You can always offer to be available if they have any questions.

Make your best effort during your last few days on the job. A positive final impression will help you later in your career.

Beating the Restructuring Blues

In the new economy, the one thing you can count on is that nothing stays the same.

Surviving and thriving in your career means learning how to manage change...

A neighbour of mine is going through a major restructuring at work. He came to me the other night feeling confused and pretty angry. I told him, if you want to stay working:

1. Co-operate with those in charge, even if you don't like what they're doing.

2. Always appear positive and optimistic. Don't keep harking back to "the good old days" or talking about "the way we used to do it."

3. Play the new game, not the old one. Find out the new goals of top management and do everything you can to help them.

4. Give the changes a chance to work!

You can beat the restructuring blues only by mastering the art of managing change.

"Headhunter"
Dos and Don'ts

OK, you get a surprise call from a headhunter.
Are you prepared?

Surviving and thriving in your career means
being ready to move on up...

Yesterday, a client came to see me. He'd just received a call from a placement agency, and he was really, really nervous. He'd never been approached by a headhunter before.

I told him: If you get the call, always be willing to discuss a new job. Contacts like this are very useful. Especially these days.

The recruiter is just putting together a short list. This first call is a kind of "test" to see if you're right for their client's needs.

Be positive, sound interested, and ask enough questions to evaluate the position.

Treat every call from a recruiter as a golden opportunity to climb the next step in your career ladder.

Installing Some Career Shock Absorbers

Everyone, no matter what their position, encounters some bumps in the road when they're working.

Surviving and thriving in your career means installing some career shock absorbers...

Job depression. It happens to everyone. The next time you start feeling depressed or start doubting yourself at work, remember these tips:

1. Always be content with doing your best, not what other people expect of you.

2. Recharge your self-esteem batteries and look for ways to celebrate and feel good about what you do.

3. Don't allow your workmates to make you feel guilty about work that you haven't completed.

4. Keep your job in perspective. It is certainly an important part of your life, but it is only a part of it!

You'll travel on your career highway a lot easier with some career shock absorbers.

Revitalizing Your Career

*Many baby boomers today
are feeling stuck in their careers.*

*Surviving and thriving in your career means
revitalizing your career...*

My sister came to me the other day. She said, "Steve, I'm frustrated and bored. I've achieved all the goals I've planned in my career."

I told her: I've been there, I know how you feel. You need a new challenge! You need to develop new skills, skills that help you find satisfaction on a new level.

Try teaching others. This will help your self-confidence, and will get you involved again.

Finally, you should find a cause outside your business that calls for time and energy and gives you a new sense of commitment.

Remember, if you feel you've "plateaued," but not "peaked," find a new challenge. You'll be happier if you do.

Turn What You Know Best into Cash

Do you want to do what you love to do and get paid for it?

Surviving and thriving in your career means turning your hobby into a paycheque...

Terrence Dickinson is one of the world's most respected astronomers. He's been looking at the night sky since he was a boy and has turned his self-taught hobby into a full-time science writing business. He's the one who wrote most of the astronomy questions for Trivial Pursuit and now he just sold the movie rights to one of his books to Steven Spielberg!

Look at your own hobbies and interests. Ask yourself —could I make money doing what I now do only for fun? Is there a way I could use what I know to fill a need in the marketplace?

If you turn what you love to do into some extra cash, you just might be able to turn it into a great new career.

Beating the
"Bad Boss Blues"

*Even if you have a bad boss,
you can still be successful in your job.*

*Surviving and thriving in your career means
beating the bad boss blues...*

When you find yourself working for a bad boss, here are some tips to consider.

If your boss hogs the credit for your work, say you prefer a team approach. If that doesn't work, send copies to others for feedback, including your boss's boss.

With a boss who asks you to be dishonest, first tell him or her you don't like it. If nothing changes, go to their boss, and tell them how you feel.

Finally, you can always "fire" your boss. Put in for a transfer, or if that fails, quit. Believe me, no job is worth all that stress and aggravation.

If you have a bad boss, you don't have to suffer in silence. Speak up and you'll beat the bad boss blues.

Attitude! Attitude! Attitude!

William James once said "Human beings can alter their lives by altering their attitudes of mind."

Surviving and thriving in your career means always staying positive...

If there's one lesson I've learned at least a thousand times, it's that attitude is the one "make or break" factor in a person's career. And, in the new economy, your attitude—the way you express your feelings about who you are and what you do at work—is even more important than ever.

Think about the importance of attitude for a moment. How many successful people do you know who constantly complain about what they do? How many people do you know who just got a big raise and spend time openly "trashing" their boss? How many people do you know who just got promoted and really hate the company they work for?

A positive attitude will help you get that new job you've been looking for, or more importantly, help you hold on to the one you've got.

Picking a New Career After Asking the Right Questions

Do you want to change your career and do something completely different?

Surviving and thriving in your career means answering some pretty important questions...

Today, more than ever, people are changing careers in search of the best moneymaking opportunities. If you're thinking of making a career change, why not find something that you love to do?

Taking a personal inventory will help. Ask yourself: What makes you happy? What are your strengths? What special skills and talents do you have? What do you do at work that gives you a sense of real accomplishment? What have you achieved at work that people have raved about?

If you're considering a career change, take the time and prepare a personal inventory. You'll make the best new career choice if you do.

The Right Way
to Resign from a Job

*There's a right way and a wrong way
to resign from a job.*

*Surviving and thriving in your career means
building bridges, not burning them...*

A friend of mine recently decided to quit her job. She'd been unhappy for months, and felt that the company had not been supporting her.

In her draft letter of resignation she described her employer's faults in detail and bitterly expressed her disappointment.

I told her, when you resign you should never burn bridges. You never know when you'll need that reference letter. Your resignation letter should only say that:

1. **You regret leaving.**

2. **You've obtained a better position.**

3. **You appreciate the support you've received.**

4. **The effective date of your resignation.**

So stick to the essentials the next time you resign from a company. Leave with grace and a professional attitude.

Begin It and the Work Will Be Completed

When you think about it,
half of getting a job done is starting it.

Surviving and thriving in your career means
making a serious start...

Ever have a day when you thought about many ideas but never did anything about them?

A friend once told me: "The only way you get the job done is to take the seat of your pants to the seat of the chair—AND GET STARTED!" Sounds simple—but it works. Facing an empty piece of paper or computer screen is a challenging experience. But it is a *start*. First beginnings are the hardest to make. The act is infinite. The end results are boundless.

Famed philosopher Goethe said it best: "Only engage, and then the mind grows heated; Begin it, and the work will be completed."

There are books written about it and Nike says it all the time. But in the end, nothing ever gets done unless you start—*so* "just do it!"

Practice Kaizen

*Improving yourself is one of the best ways
I know to protect your career.*

*Surviving and thriving in your career means
practicing kaizen...*

The Japanese call it *kaizen*—adopting a philosophy of continuous improvement.

Applied to business, kaizen can be defined as the relentless quest for a better way to build a higher quality product or service. Applied to people, it's a commitment to keep reaching higher and higher, pushing to do better and better, always striving to improve what you have to offer.

Think about it. If you increase your skills, knowledge, and performance, bit by bit, week in week out, it will add up to a big competitive advantage in two or three years.

Remember, "practice kaizen." You'll get better at a faster rate than your competitors if you do.

"We're All in This, Alone"

Comedienne Lily Tomlin once joked:
"We're all in this, alone."

Surviving and thriving in your career means
becoming a job entrepreneur...

In the new economy, it's smart career management to start thinking and acting like you're in business for yourself, even though you may be working for someone else.

Bosses appreciate people who arrive at work with an entrepreneurial attitude, eager to serve customers better, improve sales, and cut expenses, especially if they do these things willingly and on their own.

Bosses also reward people who take responsibility for the success of the entire company, rather than just their own job.

Turn yourself into a "job entrepreneur." You'll stay employed longer and get paid more if you do.

part FOUR

How to Develop a Positive Attitude and Build a Successful Career

L ife is 90% attitude. Approaching your work (and your life!) with the right attitude is vitally important. But attitude is an intangible, shifting target that is difficult to define and improve.

These scripts suggest that those who are curious, enthusiastic, and dedicated are the ones most likely to succeed. If you are always learning, always wanting to do your best, and caring about what you do, then your attitude is likely to be positive.

If you have a personal vision, if you know where you're going, and have a structure and a context for your life, then your attitude is likely to be positive.

These scripts are a series of inspirations illustrating how your attitude can be more positive. Attitude can't be taught like mathematics, but you can learn by example and illustration how to bring a better outlook to your career and your life.

Do You Have a
Mission Statement?

*Most successful companies have
a Mission Statement. Do you?*

*Surviving and thriving in your career means
committing to a Mission Statement...*

M any people often fail when they have no purpose... no Mission Statement.

Internationally respected leadership authority Stephen
Covey believes everyone should have a statement, and
reminds us that our Mission Statement should focus on
what we want to be and what we want to do. This Mission Statement also sets out the values and principles
that we will use to get there.

It is fundamentally important that we have a purpose in
life and that we are willing to fine-tune it. Finding that
purpose may be hard work, but it is the key benchmark
of personal and professional success!

If you haven't already done so, write your Mission Statement and share it with the people you care about.

The Hidden Secret of Career Success

Do you know the hidden secret of career success?

Surviving and thriving in your career means always believing you can do it...

I read a great story the other day, about four young women who became one of the world's most successful recording groups.

In 1962, this group began performing in their church and doing small concerts. Then came their chance to cut a record. It was a flop. Later, they recorded another—it flopped too. Their third, fourth, fifth, sixth, seventh, eighth, yes, even their ninth recordings failed.

Early in 1964, they managed to get booked on the Dick Clark Show, but even that exposure didn't help them. Then, later that summer they released "Where Did Our Love Go?" This song rocketed to the top of the charts, and Diana Ross & The Supremes have been stars ever since.

So remember this Motown success story. Never give up on yourself, or on your dreams to succeed.

Goose Power— Nothing to Honk About!

When geese migrate south,
they teach us a powerful lesson!

Surviving and thriving in your career means
thinking and acting like a goose!...

Ever wonder why geese fly in a "V" formation? By doing so, the whole flock adds over 70% greater flying range than if each bird flew solo. Now that's teamwork.

When people work together for a common cause there's a sense of community and a propulsion— because everyone is headed in the same direction.

There's no question—there is strength in numbers and a power in shared experiences. No question, if everyone is headed in the same direction—for the same purpose and the same goal—nothing can stop them!

Next time you take a gander at geese in "V" formation imagine how humans could benefit from their glorious example of working together!

Know How to
Fail Successfully

*People in business today can learn a lot
from major league baseball players.*

*Surviving and thriving in your career means
knowing how to fail, successfully...*

A depressed CEO came to see me for some advice
the other night. "Steve," he said, "I am a complete
failure. Half the time I don't succeed in doing what's
best for the company."

I picked up my 1970 *New York Times Almanac*, opened
it to a well worn page, and asked him to read the list of
the lifetime batting averages of the world's greatest
baseball players, led by Ty Cobb.

The CEO paused and said: "Ty Cobb—.367. That's it?"

"Yes," I said. "Think about it. Ty Cobb got a hit once
out of every three times at bat. He didn't even bat .500,
yet he was tremendously successful."

You can't be successful at everything you do. You have
to accept that you will fail, at least part of the time.

Growth Opens the Door to the Circle of Life

Growth is the key that gives us power in our circle of life!

Surviving and thriving on the job means growing into our confident selves...

Many of us were touched by the poignant story of Disney's now famous *Lion King*. We all remember how the baby lion cub grew to become a majestic king of the jungle.

In many ways, we resemble the cub—as a helpless infant, then a clumsy, unsure youngster, and finally a confident adult.

The lion grew to become king because he took his training and learned to lead others. By acquiring our own set of skills, emotional maturity, and a strong spiritual direction, each day brings us closer to leading in our own circle of life.

There are many keys in life. The one that opens the most doors is growth.

The Secret to the Right Path

Some people ask Why?
—while others ask "Why Not?"

Surviving and thriving in your career means
using the freedom to choose...

Famed psychiatrist Victor Frankl once wrote: "The last of the human freedoms is to choose one's attitudes."

Frankl should know it best. During World War II he was imprisoned in a concentration camp for years with only his thoughts as a friend. It was his attitude that caused his mind to be free while his body was held captive.

Depending on your attitude, a mountain could look majestic and magical or it could be perceived to be intimidating and unsafe. How we approach the mountain, how we end up viewing it, is in the attitude we choose to take.

To choose the right path in life we must choose the right attitude! Who knows? Your mountain may be there for the taking!

Accentuate the Positive

*Think of at least one positive thing
that's happened to you in the past 24 hours!*

*Surviving and thriving in your career means
making a shift to the positive...*

Famous motivator Leo Buscaglia questioned: "Why do some people always see beautiful skies and lovely flowers and incredible human beings—while others are hard-pressed to find anything or any place that is beautiful?"

I once took a train to New York City. As we travelled, I was appalled at the garbage and the graffiti on the cement walls along the way. I was also captivated by the tiny flowers and plants that were strong enough to sneak through the tunneled pavement and flourish in just a tiny bit of sunlight. Positive beauty in anything is certainly in the eyes of the beholder.

Take a lesson from the tiny flower: Accentuate the positive and look at the bright side of life!

Treat Your Mind
Like a Garden

Ever consider your mind as a garden? All it needs are some positive seeds and tender loving care.

Surviving and thriving in your career means taking care of the garden of your mind...

A person's mind can be compared to a summer garden—it can be intelligently cultivated or allowed to run rampant.

We must tend to our mental gardens—edging out negative thoughts—weeding out those destructive and defeating habits.

As the master of your garden, you have the option to plant good seeds, nurture the plants, and receive positive results.

Like a garden, a person's mind needs tender, loving care so it can yield positive thoughts, careful understanding, and bountiful success. Do a little weeding and give your mind a chance to grow!

Your mind, like a garden, can be positively cultivated or allowed to run wild. The option is yours!

Are You Laying Bricks—
Or Building Cathedrals?

*Take pride in knowing that those
"little" things you do help make big things happen!*

*Surviving and thriving in your career means
understanding the bigger picture...*

On the Cathedral grounds, a London tourist—spotting two bricklayers—asked the first: "My good man, what are you building?" He retorted: "Building a wall!" And to the second bricklayer, "What about you?" "I'm finishing off the back altar of the Cathedral—for the glory of God. It will be strong and true and last for generations!"

It was obvious that the second bricklayer had a more pronounced purpose—knowing that what he was doing was part of a much bigger picture!

We seem to do so many little things that apparently "don't count"—never taking pride in the end result. Think about it: Are you just laying bricks or are you building cathedrals?

Be proud of the "little things" you do... knowing that you've contributed significantly to the overall effort.

Believe in the Believers

Strong, successful role models can be excellent yardsticks for your personal improvement.

Surviving and thriving in your career means looking for good influences...

As a kid, most of us had role models—entertainers, sports figures, teachers, a coach, or even a relative.

As an adult, we need role models too—perhaps a manager, a friend, or a co-worker. We have a chance to study them, model after them, compete with them, and even outdo them.

As we gain a certain status in our lives these role models may change. Nothing's wrong with that. It's a perfect way to measure our progress, be proud of our accomplishments, and feel good about our achievements.

If you're going to pick role models—believe in the achievers. Aim high and practice what they've preached!

Love the Stuff You Do!

*If you're not happy or proud of your job
—why are you doing it?*

*Surviving and thriving in your career means
taking pride in your position...*

I once met a man at the airport in Cleveland, Ohio. It
seemed as though I'd watched him for hours. He
was shining shoes. That's right—shining shoes.

I learned after talking with him that he'd been in the
shoe-shine business for years and loved it. He said he
was making a good living and he was proud to give the
best shine in the city.

I was genuinely impressed by this craftsman who could
teach a few things to a lot of big corporations (and
junior executives, too)—service, dignity, pride, and a
desire to be the best.

Next time you're looking for success in what you do,
first find something you're proud of and love to do.
Life can't get better than that!

Winners Visualize Success

*If you picture something positive happening,
it's more likely it will happen.*

*Surviving and thriving in your career means
seeing yourself successful...*

D r. Rob Gilbert once said "losers visualize the penalties of failure—winners visualize the rewards of success!"

Some people constantly think of driving that new car, taking that exciting holiday, buying a special house (even getting a new job)—only to get stopped in their tracks because of negative thinking.

If we cannot visualize the positive things in life, how can we make our dreams come true? Put yourself in a new car, take a fancy vacation, get a new job, and benefit from the rewards of your dreams! Only you can do it.

Picture yourself enjoying the rewards of your dreams! Visualize and make those dreams come true!

You Are What You Think

We've all heard "You are what you eat"
but how about "You are what you think?"

Surviving and thriving in your career means
choosing the right mental diet...

James Allen, in his book *As a Man (or Woman) Thinketh*,
spells out the formula for success in every human
endeavor.

He says: "The mind guides our footsteps as we progress
along the pathway of life... we can only rise, conquer and
achieve by lifting up our thoughts and then our deeds."
So simply put... so profoundly significant! Good
thoughts and deeds can never produce bad results.

Take an inventory of how you think and what you
think. Does this inventory match up to your goals and
expectations? You may have to do some fine-tuning but
it's a small price to pay to get to the top!

Good thoughts and deeds can never produce bad
results.

Our Greatest Gift is Today

Everything we need to achieve success
can start today!

Surviving and thriving in your career means
taking advantage of every waking hour today...

In *Gone With the Wind*, Scarlett said: "There's always tomorrow." In real life many people count on too many tomorrows—delaying their needs, wants, desires, and growth!

We are given one precious day at a time to put our lives, our dreams, and our achievements into action! Yesterdays are gone and tomorrows may never come! Our greatest gift is today—a day in which we can begin.

Think about what you want to discover, want to accomplish, want to improve on—then act today! Like the saying goes, "Don't put off till tomorrow, what you can do today!"

Why procrastinate—when everything you want can be put into practice today?

You Can't Go Forward
with Your Brakes On

*If your life isn't moving in a positive,
forward direction—you'd better find out
what's holding you back.*

*Surviving and thriving in your career means
taking your foot off the brake pedal...*

Ever hit your car's accelerator only to find you've
left the emergency brake on?

Sociologist Kurt Lewin has developed a concept called
Force Field Analysis. In it he describes two kinds of
forces: **restraining forces** that discourage forward move-
ment and **driving forces** that cause you to move along.

Some people go through life with their brakes on holding
themselves back with procrastination, fear, and negative
thinking. Others release those brakes and drive forward—
positively, logically, and confidently. Who do you think is
more successful?

Are you moving in the right direction—or is your life at
a standstill? Take a lesson from the car and check your
brakes.

Optimism: The Secret Ingredient for Success

*Every cloud has a silver lining—
in order to succeed, you have to discover it.*

*Surviving and thriving in your career means
drinking from the full half of your glass...*

The dictionary defines "optimism" as "a tendency to look on the brighter side of things... a belief that everything will turn out for the best."

Historically things have improved because people are optimistic. They look for a good today and a powerful, positive tomorrow. And because of it, optimism has always generated successful "possibilities" for progress.

So many changes are happening and so many people will rise to a certain power because they are optimistic. So—is your glass half full or half empty? All depends on your desire to succeed!

When you think you're down and out, look at life from a positive perspective—try some optimism—success is sure to follow!

Every Morning is a New Gift

Every morning is a new gift.
Learn to value it wisely!

Surviving and thriving in your career means
serving yourself a full-course breakfast for your mind...

We all begin our days in different ways. Some stumble out of bed or lunge for a coffee. Others start by running and exercising—getting those muscles in shape.

Exercising is important, but don't forget one of the most important parts of your body—your mind. More and more people are pausing to experience some daily personal moments by reading, listening to a positive motivational tape, or being silently enthusiastic—just looking at nature. By giving your mind a workout, you put both your body and mind in perfect balance and it sets you up for a successful day.

So tomorrow morning, take a little time and present yourself a gift. Quietly do some "Spiritual Calisthenics." Then celebrate this day and be glad and successful in it!

Success Starts with Setting the Right Goals

Setting goals helps you in so many ways—it brings you closer to achievement and personal reward!

Surviving and thriving in your career means starting with the right goals...

A lot of people have a flare for "acting out" success, but only those who have goals seem to be the ones who make it.

What are your goals? Where do you want to be? One common desire we all have is to make more money, but money isn't necessarily a goal. HOW you'll make the money, WHERE you'll make the money, and WHEN you plan to use the money—these are more reasonable goals to consider.

Setting goals gives you a chance to get where you want to go. It's a flight plan for personal and professional success.

Write your goals down today! Set your purpose, focus your energy, develop a plan, and you'll reap the reward!

How to Avoid Stress

Incredibly, North Americans take over twelve million sleeping tablets every night.

Surviving and thriving in your career means knowing how to avoid stress...

Because of tremendous stress in today's work world, many people don't sleep peacefully, or long enough.

An old boss of mine enjoyed ten hours of sleep every night, and once shared his "sleep secrets" with me:

1. Find work that you truly love to do.

2. Develop systems and a plan for your work, then make sure you follow them.

3. Don't fall into the trap of thinking that you alone are responsible for carrying the world on your shoulders.

4. Never take yourself or your job too seriously.

Learning how to avoid stress is critically important if you want to succeed, sleep well, and stay healthy.

The Ten Commandments of Self-Confidence

*The strength of a person's belief
in who they are and what they can achieve
can create extraordinary success.*

*Surviving and thriving on the job means
following the ten commandments of self-confidence...*

Dr. Judith Briles has mastered her way to the top in every field she's chosen, from stockbroker to financial planner to author and broadcaster, by following her "Ten Commandments of Self-Confidence":

1. To your own self be true.
2. Create positive thinking.
3. Know that you're not alone.
4. Learn something new.
5. Assess the situation and be realistic.
6. Take credit for your accomplishments.
7. Aspire higher.
8. Get some feedback.
9. Take care of yourself.
10. Stay in circulation.

If you believe in yourself and your goals, you'll have mastered the secret to career success.

Making the Impossible Possible

Winston Churchill once said:
"Never, never, never, never give up."

Surviving and thriving in your career means
making the impossible possible...

History teaches us that the most famous achievers won because they refused to be discouraged by defeat.

Consider the story of Louis L'Amour, author of over 100 western novels with over 200 million copies in print. He received 350 rejections from publishers before he finally sold his first book!

Thomas Edison tried over 2,000 experiments before he finally got his new light bulb to work. He later told a reporter: "I never failed once. Inventing a light bulb just happened to be a 2,000-step process."

Great things are achieved by people who dream great things and never give up.

Say "Yes" to Life!

The key to high personal performance
is to say "Yes!" to life.

Surviving and thriving in your career means
knowing what you want...

Peter Jensen, in his book *The Inside Edge*, writes about the importance of having a personal vision. He says vision is the power switch, the energy that helps us find motivation in everyday life. For example, what motivates an Olympic performer is not the boring routine of endless practice, it's the dream of Olympic gold.

The secret to a personal vision is to answer two questions: "What do I really want in life?" and "What do I need for happiness?"

High performers make full use of their unique gifts and are faithful to their dream—they don't follow the crowd, they follow their own inner vision.

Craft yourself a personal vision and be all you can be. It's the only way to have a successful career.

"The Victor"

Your attitude is the fuel that drives your career.

Surviving and thriving in your career means always believing in yourself...

I treasure this poem. Although it was written years ago, I believe passionately in its message:

> *If you think you are beaten, you are.*
> *If you think you dare not, you don't.*
> *If you like to win, but think you can't,*
> *It's almost a cinch you won't.*
> *If you think you'll lose... you're lost.*
> *For out in the world we find*
> *Success begins with a fellow's will.*
> *It's all in the state of mind.*
> *Life's battles don't always go*
> *To the stronger or faster man.*
> *But sooner or later, the man who wins*
> *Is the man who thinks he can.*

You must believe in yourself before you can make your dreams come true.

Lessons from *Hamlet*

*Shakespeare certainly understood
the effect stress can have on people.*

*Surviving and thriving in your career means
learning from a 15th century playwright...*

R emember Hamlet? Talk about stress! His mother
and uncle were an item, his fiancée went to a
watery grave, and every night his father's ghost hound-
ed him to take action. He talked to himself a lot, but
did nothing to help himself.

In the end Hamlet realized "there is nothing good or bad
but thinking makes it so." In other words, our attitude
determines whether events work for us or against us.

I always tell my clients to try and focus on the here and
now. Don't forget to laugh, and don't forget that life is
still fun!

Attitude is everything—only you can turn a "negative"
into a "positive."

When Managed Well, It's All "Small Stuff"

Dr. Hans Selye said: "Although we can't avoid stress, we sure can minimize it!"

Surviving and thriving in your career means turning big stuff into small stuff...

When you think about it, life is largely a process of adapting to positive (and negative) situations. Whether it's losing a job or getting a promotion, we're always being called upon to "adapt" to change. Your happiness and health depend on how successful you are at managing the stress around that change.

Here are five tips that will help:

1. **Always allow an extra 15 minutes to get to appointments.**
2. **Learn how to say No!**
3. **Simplify your work day.**
4. **Make friends with "non-worriers."**
5. **Relax your standards. The world won't end if your desk doesn't get cleaned off until tomorrow.**

Stress doesn't always have to be "Big Stuff." When managed well, it's all "Small Stuff"!!!

What is Life?

Successful people start each day
wanting to do great things.

Surviving and thriving in your career means
living each day to the fullest...

Each morning I'm reminded of the importance of making every day count. That's because I've posted a poem entitled *What is Life?* on my fridge, a poem that's helped me many times in my career. Here are a couple of lessons from it:

Life is an adventure...dare it

Life is beauty...praise it

Life is opportunity...take it

Life is a song...sing it

Life is a goal...achieve it

Life is a mission...fulfill it

You've gotta make the most of every day and most of all, you've gotta live with passion and purpose.

Take Personal Time-Outs

*You'll perform better on the job
if you relax more off the job.*

*Surviving and thriving in your career means
taking personal time outs...*

The book *Timeshifting* by Stephan Rechtschaffen offers some great advice on how to create more time to enjoy your life. It's based on the old credo: the more you enjoy life, the more you'll enjoy your job.

1. Find at least 30 minutes every day to do nothing.

2. Don't fill up your entire calendar each day. Schedule some "unplanned" thinking time.

3. Make time to do what you really like to do.

4. Take at least two weeks a year to truly relax. Do the things on vacation that you want to do, not the things you have to do.

Schedule personal time-outs to stay fresh and relaxed. You'll cope better in today's high stress workplace if you do.

You Gotta Take that First Step

*Do your unsolved problems
keep piling higher and higher?*

*Surviving and thriving on the job means
taking the first step toward solutions...*

Successful people know that beginning something is half of doing it. A friend of mine who's a psychiatrist told me that she considers her patients' problems half-solved when they make their first appointment.

The reason? Well, she's found that new patients have usually been considering therapy for years. When they call and make an appointment, it's because they have finally decided to get started solving their problems. Applying this thinking to business is simple: start the project and it's half finished.

You can cut your problems in half by taking that first step to solve them.

It's How You Do It
that Counts

*Jim Leyland, the manager of the
World Series winning Florida Marlins,
said "It's been a long time coming."*

*Surviving and thriving in your career means
always doing your best...*

Bill Clennan, a well known public speaker, has a way
of living that has propelled him to the top of his field.

He's converted his philosophy into a poem which basi-
cally says that the real prize of any contest is not just
simply winning, it's learning how to win.

In trying to win, you build a skill,
You learn that winning depends on will.

You never grow by how much you win,
You only grow by how much you put in.

So any new challenge, you've just begun,
Put forth your best, and you've already won.

It's not what you do, it's how you do it that counts.

You Gotta Avoid Toxic People

A 100,000 volt positive charge
does you little good if you surround yourself
with a million watts of negativity.

Surviving and thriving in your career means
avoiding toxic people...

Many people live each day miserable and depressed, but never do anything to change.

I'm reminded of the story of a dog sitting on a porch moaning and groaning. A young girl walked by and asked the dog's owner why it was acting that way. "Because he's lying on a nail," the owner replied. "So, why doesn't he move?" asked the girl. The owner paused, smiled and said, "Because it's not hurting enough."

The lesson is simple. There are two types of people in life: those who'll drag you down by complaining about problems and those who'll help you grow by solving problems.

Don't become a victim of the negative syndrome. Avoid "toxic people" and you'll get where you want to go.

Take Control
of Your Destiny

*Every day, literally thousands of people
blame their troubles on somebody else.*

*Surviving and thriving in your career means
taking control of your destiny...*

General Electric is the tenth largest industrial corpo-
ration in the world. Its leader, Jack Welch, runs the
company on the basis of a few tough, but simple, rules.

1. **Face reality as it is, not as it was or as you wish
   it were.**

2. **Change before you have to.**

3. **Control your own destiny, or someone else will.**

Over the past few years I've learned that high performance leaders like Welch take control and believe
strongly that they have the power to change their lives.

Don't blame others for your problems—take charge of
yourself and make something happen to better your
future.

E Stands for Enthusiasm!

"Nothing ever succeeds which exuberant spirits have not helped to produce."

Surviving and thriving in your career means being infectiously enthusiastic...

I learned long ago that an enthusiastic attitude could be one of my best friends at work. This lesson is even more important in today's re-engineered world. Let's face it: A genuine display of good old-fashioned enthusiasm can often mean the difference between getting the order or losing it, between getting a job or losing it, and most importantly, between keeping your job or losing it.

When I was shopping around my book proposal to different publishers, I was lucky enough to have three companies eager to sign me. The publisher I chose was the one who showed the most enthusiasm about my work.

E stands for enthusiasm. Make yours genuine and infectious!

Turning Bad Times into Good

Les Brown once said: "When you endure and persevere, you've positioned yourself to grow and succeed."

Surviving and thriving on the job means turning bad times into good ones...

I read a moving story about someone who turned a terrible personal tragedy into a tremendous achievement.

In 1980, Candy Lightener's daughter was struck and killed by a drunken driver. Candy's grief turned to rage when her daughter's killer was sentenced to only two years in prison.

Upset by the legal system, Candy organized Mothers Against Drunk Drivers (MADD), and has since convinced government after government to pass tougher laws against drunk driving.

As a result of her daughter's death, Candy has realized a far greater vision in her life than she ever thought possible.

When times are tough in your career, it's time for you to get going and make something positive happen.

Take Some
Laughter Tonic

Aristotle once said
"Laughter is a bodily exercise precious to health."

Surviving and thriving in your career means
never taking yourself too seriously...

There are dozens of studies that show when people laugh enough each day, they put their emotions on a more optimistic track and their negative feelings begin to lift.

A few years ago, a friend of mine, seriously ill in the hospital, decided to move home where he treated himself to what he called "laugh therapy." After watching old "I Love Lucy" and Carol Burnett shows, he found that ten minutes of belly laughter would give him two hours of pain free sleep. I've found that even five minutes of laughter makes my most difficult customer seem not so difficult anymore.

Whether you're at the top of the ladder or climbing your way up, laughter is one of life's most important treasures.

Dream and Dream Big

*The poet Percy Shelley once wrote
"We might be all we dream."*

*Surviving and thriving in your career means
daring to dream, then dreaming big...*

There are a lot of people in the world who believe that dreaming is a folly and that we shouldn't dream because dreaming won't get you anywhere.

I believe the opposite is true. Dreaming can make life a truly wonderful and meaningful experience.

Take Margot Page, for example. The three-time women's hockey world champion decided last year, after retiring from the game, that she wanted to pursue a career as a hockey coach and professional broadcaster. Now, she's landed a job as the coach of the Niagara University NCAA hockey team and does colour commentary on TSN!

Margot's secret? Well, she once told me that she dares to dream, dreams big, and then works "her butt off" to make her dreams come true.

You have to dream to create a motivating target to shoot for. Dream big and you'll surprise a lot of people —maybe even yourself—with what you can accomplish.

When All Else Fails,
Just "Go For It"

The movie **Scream** *is a rags-to-riches story for writer Kevin Williamson.*

Surviving and thriving in your career means pulling out all the stops and just going for it...

I read a great "rags-to-riches" story the other day... about how 31-year-old Kevin Williamson just made it big time in the movie business. Williamson, a failed actor and playwright, was just about to have his car repossessed and desperately needed $10,000 to cover his debts. So, he decided to write a movie script called *Scream*, hoping to raise some quick cash by selling the script to a Hollywood filmmaker.

Williamson spent three days on the first draft, and then sent it to his agent. The next week it was the object of a bidding war, and he ended up with a package worth more than $500,000, plus a deal to direct a film and write two others.

Overnight successes don't just "happen," you need to "go for it" and make them happen.

The Cowboy's Story

*If you're going to be successful, you've got to be
totally focussed on achieving your goals.*

*Surviving and thriving in your career means
following the "Ya Gottas for Success."*

I just finished reading *A 2nd Helping of Chicken Soup for
the Soul* by Jack Canfield and Mark V. Hansen. In the
book the authors tell the story of a 22-year old cowboy
who started selling telephone systems with absolutely no
experience.

Within three years, he owned half the company and by
the time he turned 26, he'd earned enough to buy three
other companies. What made the cowboy a success was
his belief in the "Ya Gottas for Success."

1. He knew what he wanted and he went after it.

2. He took action to make things different.

3. He took responsibility for himself.

4. He stayed with it even when the going got tough.

5. He cared.

6. He started every day expecting to be a winner!

If you follow the "Ya Gottas for Success," you too can
live the life of your dreams.

Taking Charge
of Your Mind

*In today's "dog eat dog" world,
a positive attitude is critical.*

*Surviving and thriving in your career means
taking charge of your mind...*

Charles Swindoll said it best: "The longer I live, the more I realize the impact of attitude on life."

"It's more important than education, money, circumstance, failure, or success. It is more important than appearance, giftedness, or skill. Yes, attitude will make or break a company or a home.

"We can't change our past or the fact that people will act in a certain way. We can't change the inevitable. The only thing we can change is our attitude."

Life is 10% what happens to you, and 90% how you react to it. We are in charge of our attitudes and our minds.

Thinking Outside the Box

*Do you have a nagging problem
that you just can't solve?*

*Surviving and thriving in your career means
thinking outside the box...*

When we're working, we usually think in a
straight line. We follow traditions that say
"This is the way it's always been done."

You know, if we always thought the same way, we'd
never have things like post-it notes or curly fries!

People who thrive in today's topsy-turvy world think
laterally, they think "outside the box"—they change
their mindset and look for ways to turn problems into
opportunities. They also approach problems in a fresh
way, throwing out negatives and doubts. They brain-
storm and are always asking "What if?"

The next time you're faced with a problem, try a completely different approach. You'll turn the "I can'ts" into
"I can."

Begin With the
End in Mind

*Author Stephen Covey coined the phrase
"Begin with the end in mind."*

*Surviving and thriving in your career means
always having a map and compass...*

L ast night a friend called looking for some advice for
her 24-year-old son who had just graduated from col-
lege and is looking for his first full-time job. "Steve," she
asked, "what's the secret to building a successful career?"

"Well," I said, "whether you're starting a career at age
24, 34, or even 54, the key to success is to 'begin with
the end in mind.'"

Ask yourself: Where do you want to go? What are your
goals in life? Then write down your answers and use
them at each turn.

For there are two types of people in the world: those
without a map and compass who are headed for
Nowheresville, and those with a well thought-out
career plan who are headed for Successville.

Being career smart is knowing what you want, writing it
down, and then committing yourself to accomplishing it.

Don't Give Up

Albert Einstein once said:
"In the middle of every difficulty lies opportunity."

Surviving and thriving in your career means never giving up on your dreams...

The other day I read the story of a woman who for years tried to land a job as a talk show host with a U.S. radio network. Nobody would hire her because nobody felt she would be able to attract a big enough audience.

She went to Puerto Rico and then to the Dominican Republic before returning to the U.S. and working as a reporter.

Life wasn't easy. She was fired 18 times before she got her big break in the talk show business.

Now, Sally Jesse Raphael is a two-time Emmy Award-winning host of her own TV talk show which reaches eight million viewers throughout Canada, the U.S., and the United Kingdom.

Sally's lesson: You should never give up on either yourself or your dreams.

The Resolution
to Succeed

Abraham Lincoln once said:
"Always bear in mind that your resolution to
succeed is more important than any other thing."

Surviving and thriving in your career means
believing you can...

Many successful people I know are quick to point out that others have talent superior to theirs. Yet they are confident they can achieve almost anything—that they literally can "control" their future—because they believe in themselves and have a passionate inner desire to succeed.

Tommy Lasorda, former manager of the Dodgers, often told his players: "Races are not won by the fastest athletes. Fights are not won by the strongest men. But the races are won and the fights are won by those who want to win most of all."

The intangible quality that always separates successful people from talented people who fail is the sheer force of their passions and wills.